Contents

The author

Rachel Pinder was a teacher for 28 years, for the last ten of which she was headteacher of Drayton Park Primary School in north London. She studied at the London School of Economics, where she gained a degree in Economics and Social Anthropology. As well as teaching at all levels in primary and secondary schools, she taught adults in prison for several years. She has been an examiner of teaching students and, since her early retirement, has been involved in working on induction programmes for probationary teachers in London. In 1979, she was awarded an Associateship of the University of London Institute of Education for her research in the area of progressive education. She is married to an artist and illustrator and they have two daughters.

To my husband, Bill Pinder, without whose unfailing support and encouragement this book would never have been written.

Preface

I hear and I forget,
I see and I remember,
I do and I understand.

The ideas in this book are not mine; they are as old as the Chinese proverb. I make, therefore, no claims for originality. My only claim is to have learned from reading what others have written, from observing how my contemporaries practised, and trying in my own teaching to incorporate all that seemed to me to assist children's learning. As part of this process, through monitoring the results of different methods in terms of children's progress, I reached certain conclusions. This book is based on what I learned.

Since I am a parent as well as a teacher, I sympathise with the concerns of parents about their children's education; my husband and I had many anxieties of our own when our daughters were pupils. So this book is an attempt to share with other parents what I have found out about the processes of education through my work as a teacher in the classroom, and as head of a primary school.

I have had generous help from many friends and colleagues who have read and criticised, lent me examples of their work with children, and given immense practical support. I would like to thank the following:

Margot Pinder for her professional work on the index; Catherine Fleischmann for her advice; Brian Simon and Nanette Whitbread for their encouragement; Laurie Buxton and John Kay for their time and helpful criticisms; Linda Lefevre and Frank Brereton for allowing me access to materials produced at Drayton Park School, and for their unfailing willingness to search out and find the things I needed; Bill Pinder for drawing the flow diagrams; Jeannie Billington, Judith Charlton, Leiria Ewart, Sheenagh Goodingham,

Simon Marsh, Marcia Thompson and Beverley Watkins for allowing me to use their work; the editors for their patience and sympathetic collaboration; my many colleagues over the past 30 years from whom I have learned so much; the children who provided the writings and drawings used in the book; and the members of my own family for their constant support and encouragement. I would also like to acknowledge a debt to all those educational writers whose ideas I have seized upon in my teaching career and quoted in this book.

Above all I am grateful to the several hundred children with whom I have had such happy contact, and to their parents, because without them I would have learned nothing.

Rachel Pinder

1 | Controversies, past and present

Progressive, exploratory, investigative, child-centred, experience-based and modern methods, these are all terms that one hears bandied about when primary education is discussed. Sometimes these are used pejoratively as they were in the *Black Papers* produced during the 1960s, which talked of 'classrooms where chaos reigns, all children doing exactly what they like.' (*Black Paper Two*, Cox and Dyson) At other times they are used positively, as good models for teachers, as they were in the Plowden Report, *Children and their Primary Schools* in 1967.

There are times when national policy appears to be in favour of these methods, as in the ten years following the Plowden Report. At other times, like the present, official voices are recommending a return to what are called traditional methods. How should parents view these shifts and what can they do to ensure that their children are getting the best possible primary education? It is especially difficult for parents to be clear about the issues involved when there are many teachers who are themselves unsure of how they should be working, and when all teachers are deeply dissatisfied both with education resourcing and with their salaries.

As a primary headteacher, with experience in primary, secondary and adult education I was particularly concerned with these issues. What kind of curriculum should be offered to the children attending our school? How much freedom should children in school have? Was the role of the teacher to help children to learn from their experience, or was it to pass on knowledge? We wanted to encourage children to write clearly and spell correctly, but without crushing their creativity. Did children learn to read best by being taught phonics, or by having stories read to them? We were concerned with the best method of introducing modern technology into the curriculum, and with the teaching of mathematics. Should children be learning tables by rote, or should they be helped to understand facts about numbers before memorising the tables? In what language did bi-lingual children learn most efficiently? We were educating children to live in a multi-ethnic society which offered the hope of equal opportunities; was our school offering good models for black children and for girls? Or did the traditional values of our society so shape the attitudes of staff that we were unwittingly maintaining a hidden curriculum which contradicted our announced policies? All these and many other questions appeared regularly on the agendas of our staff meetings, as they do in many schools.

And what of the methods we used: did they come into the category of 'modern'? If so, ought they to become more traditional? But traditional methods involved a formality and rigidity which had not featured in the school for a very long time. Should children not be allowed to pursue topics which interested them and which they enjoyed learning about? We were a school community which viewed the pupils as younger partners: pupil observers even attended governors' meetings and reported their impressions back to the older part of the school. Did this mean we were progressive, and was that then a bad thing to be? Our pupils seemed to enjoy coming to school and displayed, on the whole, enthusiasm for learning. Some parents even complained that they had difficulty in keeping a child at home when he or she was sick, and children were sometimes brought to school unfit and had to be persuaded to accompany their parents home again.

Looking at our school objectively it seemed to combine elements of many methods. Could a school be traditional and progressive at the same time? I resolved to discover more about the origins of this controversy because it seemed to me that these dichotomies which were constantly being debated directed attention away from the real needs of our pupils. There was much confusion. 'Progressive' was used very loosely: instead of using the criterion of a child making progress, many teachers styled themselves 'progressive' as a philosophical justification for woolly thinking and to avoid any obligation to self-criticism: such teachers were harming education by bringing the term into disrepute in the eyes of the public. And the public seemed to associate private education with higher standards and 'tradition'. I knew that, apart from there being a tremendous variation between the best and worst fee-paying schools, some of them did in fact offer progressive methods of teaching.

Since modern methods were under attack it seemed only sensible to find out when these methods first began to be used; how recent were they in fact? If modern methods meant organising schools so that children could learn from their own experience, did this begin perhaps in the 18th century with the philosopher Rousseau, who has been singled out as the source of progressive ideas in modern education? But more than a hundred years before Rousseau a teacher called Hezekiah Woodward wrote:

> Tell him of sharp and sweet. He will not be satisfied till he have the thing, be it grapes or vinegar, apples or honey, sugar, etc. Now he knows his adjective no man better. He relishes it on his tongue's end.

Here is a 17th century teacher claiming that children's language learning has its basis in their sensory experience, a belief endorsed by very many teachers today.

Another 17th century teacher, John Amos Comenius, emphasised learning by doing, another 'modern' idea:

> Craftsmen do not hold their apprentices down to theories; they put them to work without delay so that they may learn to forge metal by forging, to carve by carving, to paint by painting, to leap by leaping. Therefore in schools let the pupils learn to write by writing, to speak by speaking, to sing by singing, to reason by reasoning, and so on, so that schools may simply be workshops in which work is done eagerly.

Even earlier, Dean Colet, who founded St Paul's School in 1510, criticised the traditions of his time and attacked teaching by rule, the formal method of teaching Latin. In his book *Aeditio*, he advised teachers not to concentrate on rules and that speaking naturally to their pupils in Latin, reading good books to them and encouraging them to speak and write in the language 'more availeth shortly to get the true eloquent speech than all the traditions, rules and precepts of masters'. This sounds remarkably like 'modern method'.

The controversy continued throughout the Tudor period. Richard Mulcaster, who also became High Master of St Paul's, complained about teachers who:

> Think it the best that boys should fruitlessly run through all the

rules learned by heart but not understood before they set themselves to the unfolding of the meaning of authors and imitating them. (*Cato Christianus*)

Before going to St Paul's, Mulcaster was headmaster of the Merchant Taylors' School where pupils were taught music and drawing. He recognised the importance of physical education, advocated the education of girls and special training for teachers: all very progressive ideas in the 16th century. Like Dean Colet he believed that children should read and write in a language before they were taught the rules of grammar. One very modern idea which he emphasised was that young children should learn to read first in their mother tongue:

We are directed by nature to read first that which we speak first and to care for that most which we ever use.

Another teacher speaking out against the formal teaching of those times was John Brinsley. He too believed children should learn, express themselves in, and understand their own language before they were taught Latin, Greek and Hebrew. In his *Ludus Literarius* he wrote:

To read and not to understand what we read is nothing else but a neglect of all good learning and a mere abuse of the means and helps to attain this same. Or if we would write or speak of any thing let us prove it but thus: if we first understand the matter well and have it perfectly in our head, whether words to express our minds will not follow as of themselves.

He maintained that if children understood what they were learning they would be able to express themselves. He also pressed for teachers to have special training and he was opposed to the harsh corporal punishment then common.

Yet another educational reformer of this time was the philosopher and statesman Francis Bacon, who wanted to encourage the study of the real world, 'the mechanical arts and sciences'. As Joan Simon makes clear in her book *Education and Society in Tudor England*, he strongly condemned scholasticism and subservience to ancient philosophy. His methods, in their emphasis on observation of the world about and scientific deduction based on those observations, have much in common with those modern methods called 'discovery' or 'investigative'.

Here, then, we have a number of teachers who lived between the 15th and 17th centuries, all of them advocating teaching philosophies and methods which we often hear called 'modern'. Was this period the origin of our 'modern method'? Were the ideas of children learning through play and from their own sensory experiences first developed in Britain 500 years ago?

In fact, as I learned, these ideas are much older. They are also drawn from educational experience throughout the ancient world. Elizabeth Lawrence, in her book, *The Origins and Growth of Modern Education*, quotes from writings going back more than 2,000 years. One example is from Plato (who lived in the 5th and 4th centuries BC):

> Enforced learning will not stay in the mind. So avoid compulsion and let your child's lessons take the form of play.

Another educator, a Roman, Quintilian, wrote in the 1st century AD about the importance of early learning, and the danger of turning children away from learning if the early experience is not enjoyable. Even in the 5th century writings of St Augustine, *On Christian Doctrine*, we find 'modern' methods being advocated:

> And, therefore, as infants cannot learn to speak, except by learning words and phrases from those who speak, why should not men become eloquent without being taught any art of speech, simply by reading and learning the speeches of eloquent men, and by imitating them as far as they can? It is just as if a man wishing to give rules for walking should warn you not to lift the hinder foot before you set down the front one, and then should describe minutely the way you ought to move the hinges of the joints and knees. For what he says is true and one cannot walk in any other way, but men find it easier to walk by executing these movements than to attend to them while they are going through them.

This is a brilliant exposition of that 'modern' idea, learning by doing!

Philosophers and educators throughout the ages have reached similar conclusions. Can it be that those who criticise modern methods simply don't know their long history? Yet the thoughts of such eminent philosophers on education should be well known. Further, if such progressive educational ideas are not really modern, but have so long a history, are they not as traditional as those methods put forward as being 'traditional'? Perhaps, rather than a split existing between traditional and progressive education, the real dichotomy is between the progressive tradition in education and another tradition: that which is directed at maintaining the status quo above all other objectives.

2 | Why don't teachers teach like they used to?

All adults have their views of school and schooling coloured by their own memories of the time when they themselves were pupils. I was very aware of this, both as class teacher and headteacher. Parents bringing young children to school for the first time sometimes appeared hostile or nervous. I soon learned to recognise that this apparent hostility arose from feelings about their own educational experiences, if those had not been happy, and that it expressed their concern for the happiness of their children. Attempts to reassure them were usually effective and most parents became more relaxed and confident about their child's well-being in the school.

But there was another side to this concern: a certain ambivalence was sometimes expressed in parental comments. While watching a class of infants engaged on a variety of tasks, chattering and moving about freely, a mother might comment: 'They certainly enjoy school, not like when I was a child. They are really very lucky'. But another comment might be: 'They just seem to be playing all the time. I worry in case they're not learning anything. Their teacher never seems to teach them like a class'. These concerns arise because many primary teachers no longer have classrooms in which children sit silently writing, copying from blackboards. The reason they don't work like this is usually because they have learned from their training and, above all, from their own experience, that children learn more when they are actively involved in the learning process.

Learning by doing

Adults will know the situation when one is engaged on a task of some kind, perhaps hammering in a nail, washing up, or filling a washing machine, and there are small children around. They will

7

be beside you, wanting to help, to get their own hands onto the hammer, into the washing-up water, filling the washing machine. The sight of small children completely engrossed in the experience of sand and water on beaches is familiar to all of us. Young children have a need to be doing things.

'We do not stop to think that the child who does not do, does not know how to do,' wrote Maria Montessori. She was a doctor in Rome when she started to be involved in the education of small children, becoming the leader of a worldwide – and still continuing – movement to provide nursery education based on children's activity. She described in her writings a scene she had witnessed in a park in Rome. A small boy was filling his pail with gravel and his nurse was becoming increasingly impatient. Misunderstanding the purpose of the activity, she put him back into his pram and completed the task herself:

> I was struck by the loud cries of the child and by the expression of protest against violence and injustice which wrote itself on his little face . . . The little boy did not wish to have the pail full of gravel; he wished to go through the motions necessary to fill it, thus satisfying a need of his own vigorous organism. The child's unconscious aim was his own self-development; not the external fact of a pail full of little stones.

Montessori was writing nearly 80 years ago; others have observed the same behaviour in young children experiencing frustration. Professor Jean Piaget, the eminent Swiss psychologist, has written that:

> A child learns very little indeed when experiments are performed for him . . . he must do them himself rather than sit and watch them done.

How often has one watched some new device, perhaps a computer or a new car, being demonstrated, itching to get hands-on experience? Even as adults, we share this need with the child, to have the first-hand experience, rather than just watch. I myself have retained only one memory from three years of physics lessons: that was the lesson in which each of us had a sheet of paper, magnets and iron filings, and could do something for ourselves, instead of craning over to watch the teacher's demonstration. With a class of more than 40 there were not very many opportunities for practical work, but that lesson has stood out in my mind for almost 50 years.

John Amos Comenius, 1592-1670 – a most modern educator

Perhaps the educator who made the most comprehensive case for learning through activity was a man called John Amos Comenius. He was a Bohemian who lived in the 17th century. Jean Piaget has written of him:

> Comenius may undoubtedly be considered as one of the precursors of the genetic idea in developmental psychology and as the founder of a system of progressive instruction adjusted to the stage of development the pupil has reached.

Comenius himself was orphaned young and did not learn to read until he was in his teens. Yet he became the foremost educator of his day. He was a member of a Protestant sect, the Moravian Brotherhood, which believed in universal equality and brotherhood in knowledge. Because of this he suffered religious persecution and was forced to move from country to country. He opened schools in different parts of Europe, before he was forced to move on yet again. But because he lived and worked in so many places, his ideas had a widespread influence during his lifetime.

He believed that an integrated approach was as essential in education as it was in scientific research. I have already quoted him, on learning by doing. For Comenius the activity of the pupil was essential to the process of education; there was no authentic activity if the pupil passively accepted adult instruction:

> Activity is when the pupil rediscovers or reconstructs truth by means of external or internal mental action, consisting in experiment or independent reasoning.

He went further than most modern educators in advising pupils to take nothing on trust:

> Proceed by stages.
>
> Examine everything oneself without abdication in the face of

adult authority – the principle known as Autopsy.

Act on one's own impulsion – the principle known as Autopraxis, with reference to all being presented to the intellect, the memory, the tongue, the hand, the pupils shall themselves seek, discover, discuss, do and repeat without slacking, by their own efforts, the teachers being left merely with the task of seeing whether what is to be done is done and done as it should be.

These principles, formulated more than 300 years ago, seem very similar to those under attack today. They are, even today, very radical. Comenius advised students to question adult authority in every respect, to investigate everything for themselves. The teachers' task was to determine what was to be done and to check that it was done properly. Of course Comenius was addressing himself to students older than those in our primary schools, but if this advice was appropriate to an older age group, how much more appropriate is it to most of the learning within the range of younger children who are so much more dependent on their first-hand experience?

Comenius might well have had a more direct and profound influence on the education system of England and Wales – in 1641 he was invited to visit England by Members of Parliament who had heard of his work. He was asked to advise on the setting up of a school system, but the outbreak of the Civil War cut short his visit. It is interesting to speculate on what might have been!

Jean Jacques Rousseau, 1712-1778 – what he really wrote

Born in Geneva, Rousseau was of Swiss, French and Italian descent. His mother died shortly after his birth and he was brought up by his watchmaker father. His schooling was irregular, and at the age of 13 he was apprenticed to an engraver, but he was harshly treated and ran away. He led an itinerant life for many years and tried a variety of occupations, including that of tutor. He was self-educated and read widely in science, philosophy, morality and literature; he also wrote music and developed a system of musical notation.

He settled in Paris in 1742, acquired a common-law wife, and fathered five children – all of whom were brought up in orphanages as foundlings! Rousseau produced essays on a wide variety of subjects, including religion. He himself had been converted to Catholicism in his youth, but reverted to Calvinism in his middle years. In his writings he attacked many 'sacred cows' of the period, and consequently, after writing *Emile*, he fled France, under threat of arrest. In his later years he suffered from insane delusions, a condition which might have been inherited. A man of brilliant gifts, he was torn by contradictory passions throughout his life. His writing was to influence many, from Byron and Shelley to the German philosopher Immanuel Kant, as well as those like Pestalozzi, who were to shape education in the years to come.

Best known for his book *The Social Contract* which was part of the ideological base for the French Revolution in 1789, he also wrote *Emile*, which described the education of a boy from infancy to adulthood. It had a catalytic and far-reaching effect on education in Europe. Indeed, Emile's education was slavishly reproduced by some, though it seems clear from his other writings that this was probably not Rousseau's intention, his object being rather to present a series of educational maxims.

Rousseau's name is often linked with absolute freedom and permissiveness, the concept of the 'noble savage' which extolled the virtues of simplicity and primitive country life, as against the artificiality of urban surroundings. But Rousseau's ideas were more complex: he wanted children to be allowed to develop as children and objected to the fashion of the time, which was to dress them and treat them as if they were miniature men and women. His reputation as an advocate of permissiveness is not borne out in *Emile*, nor in his other works dealing with education. The children in his books are tightly circumscribed and manipulated to learn the lessons which their elders wish them to learn. Rousseau presents himself as the tutor who guides Emile to maturity. While the very beginning of the book describes an idealised primitive society which no doubt gave rise to the popular idea of him as the originator of a 'back to nature' philosophy, he went on to elaborate very structured and disciplined educational systems in his writings.

In *Emile* he wrote about the needs of the very young infant:

At the commencement of life when the memory and imagination are as yet inactive, the child is only attentive to that which actually affects the senses. His sensations are the first data upon which he can build knowledge and understanding.

And in relation to the constant activity of the young child:

> It is only by movement that we acquire an understanding of
> things which are separate from ourselves and it is only by our
> own movement that we acquire the idea of distance.

This idea is easily tested: watch a young baby reaching for an
object; many attempts have to be made before the child learns to
correlate hand and eye. Car drivers have to gain experience before
gaining the confidence to drive their cars through gaps which more
experienced drivers can assess instantly.

He applied his observations of children's movements to the
teaching of mathematics:

> Anything that brings unconstrained movement of the body
> comes easily to children. There are therefore many ways of
> interesting them in measuring, noticing and estimating
> distances. There is a very tall cherry tree; how shall we gather
> the cherries? Will the ladder in the barn be long enough? There
> is a very wide stream, how are we going to get across? Will one
> of the planks in the yard span it from side to side? We would
> like to fish in the moats of the chateau from our windows; what
> ought to be the length of our line? I want to make a swing
> attached to two trees; will a rope 12 feet in length be sufficient
> for this? I'm told that our room in the next house will be 25 feet
> square; do you think this will suit? Is it larger than our present
> room? We are extremely hungry; there are two villages; which
> of the two can we reach soonest and so eat? And so on.

It was not that Emile was not going to learn arithmetic, he simply
was not going to work second hand, from books. He would be
required to solve real problems which affected him directly. In
chapter 7, which examines modern mathematical teaching, the
approaches recommended by the Cockcroft Committee which was
set up to improve the teaching of mathematics – and whose report
Mathematics Counts was published in 1982 – can be seen to be
remarkably similar to those advocated by Rousseau.

This principle was to apply to all aspects of Emile's education:

> Teach your scholar to observe the phenomena of nature; you
> will soon rouse his curiosity, but if you would have it grow, do

not be in too great a hurry to satisfy this curiosity. Put the problems before him and let him solve them himself. Let him know nothing because you have told him but because he has learnt it for himself . . .

You wish to teach this child geography and you provide him with globes, spheres and maps. What elaborate preparations! What is the use of all these symbols; why not begin by showing him the real thing so that he may at least know what you are talking about? . . .

His geography will begin with the town he lives in . . . Let him make his own map, a very simple map, at first containing only two places; others may be added from time to time, as he is able to estimate their distance and position.

This is, of course, the kind of approach used by primary teachers today when developing environmental studies with their children.

There are some humorous examples given to illustrate how the young Emile would be taught to get up on time, or take more exercise. Of the former, Rousseau wrote:

When I wish him to awaken at an appointed time I shall tell him that at six o'clock I am going fishing or taking a walk to some spot or other and would he like to go. He consents and requests that I wake him; I promise or do not as the need seems to be. If he wakes too late he finds I have departed. There is something very wrong if he does not soon learn to wake of his own accord.

Thus Emile's education was tightly controlled in every respect; it was the very opposite of permissive – but it *was* firmly based on Emile's first-hand experience.

Johann Heinrich Pestalozzi, 1746-1827 – a father-figure

Pestalozzi was so influenced by Rousseau's ideas that he attempted for a time to bring up his own son in the manner described. His own work has been highly influential for more than 200 years and his name is known to many because of the Children's Villages named after him. The characteristic which shines out of his writings is a love for all children, for childhood itself. He was fatherless and had the misfortune to attend some dreadful schools. In one, he remembered, during an earthquake, 'the tall masters leapt down the school stairs over our heads like giants among Lilliputians'.

No wonder his sympathies were always with the many poor orphans and working children. He wrote in 1776:

> I have been struck by the misery of children placed with peasants by the parish. I have seen them crushed by hard selfishness and left for the most part without spirit and energy, I might almost say without life in body or soul.

He spent his whole life organising schools for the children of the poor. In the course of this he observed the ways in which children learned and remembered what they had learned. He realised that this happened most easily when the language used with children was rooted in some practical activity. He gives examples of this in his book *Leonard and Gertrude*:

> She never adopted the tone of instructor toward her children, she did not say to them, 'Child this is your head, your nose, your hand, your finger' . . . but instead she would say 'Come here child, I will wash your little hands' and 'I will comb your hair'. . . The verbal instruction vanished in the activity in which it had its source.

Pestalozzi believed that the child should be actively involved in education: 'Let the child not only be acted upon but let him be an agent in intellectual education'. He constantly spoke out against verbosity in education:

> The mode of doing this is not by any means to talk much *to* a child but to enter into conversation *with* a child, not to address to him many words however familiar and well chosen, but to bring *him* to express *himself* on the subject; not to exhaust the subject but to question the child about it and to let him find out and correct the answer.

It is this involvement of the child in education which is so often referred to as 'modern'. Yet it was not particularly modern, even in the 18th century!

How *did* teachers teach?

Since we have written evidence, from the dawn of history, that there were recognised controversies in education between the advocates of teaching by rule and those concerned with making teaching more effective, it must be conceded that there are at least two traditions. And since teachers like Mulcaster, Brinsley and Woodward were advocating in the books they wrote such modern ideas as matching tasks to the age of the child, using the mother-tongue, and making use of the child's sensory experiences in learning, it would seem logical to deduce that many other teachers in this country were familiar with these ideas and practices. The writing of St Augustine, from an even earlier period, confirms that learning by doing is not modern. The work of Comenius outlines schemes which contain extremely progressive ideas and clearly makes nonsense of the idea that progressive education stems from Rousseau in the 18th century. So, too, first-hand reading of Rousseau's own writings demonstrates that his ideas were far from advocating the absolute permissiveness so often attributed to him.

The question 'Why don't teachers teach like they used to?' cannot be answered without first asking 'Which teachers do you mean?' since teaching of a kind we call 'progressive' has been advocated and carried out for centuries. When one also realises that what is referred to as 'traditional' is invariably the *maintenance* tradition, the 'what was good enough for me is good enough for my child' approach, it is clear that the whole history of the *developmental* or progressive tradition in education has been completely over-looked.

The spread of the modern method

Pestalozzi's schools in Switzerland were visited by many, many teachers and educational reformers. Some, like Madame de Stael and Thomas Day, wrote books popularising his ideas. John Synge brought Pestalozzi's ideas into the British Isles and opened a school in Ireland. One person who was influenced was Charles Mayo who himself became a pupil of Pestalozzi and later, together with his sister Elizabeth, opened a school in Epsom. This was so successful that it had to move to larger premises in Cheam. Another school was opened at Ham Common, by J.P.Greaves. One visitor there, Dr James Kay, later Sir James Kay-Shuttleworth, became Secretary to the Privy Council Committee for Education. He was then in a position to give official sanction to some of Pestalozzi's ideas, which were introduced into the curriculum.

In 1836 the Mayos, together with J.P. Greaves and J.S. Reynolds, formed the Home and Colonial Infant School Society. They opened a training college in Holborn and by 1843 this was training 100 infant teachers a year. The effects of the work of the college was clear to Her Majesty's Inspectorate (HMI) which compared the more modern infant schools and the rest where the teachers' lack of training was deplored. The college qualified for a government grant in 1846.

Robert Owen, 1771-1858 – a pioneer of infant schools

A mill owner who was nevertheless a socialist, Owen had established a school for the children of his employees before he visited Pestalozzi in 1818. The school was part of Owen's model factory village in New Lanark, Scotland, which included homes for his workers, canteens, recreational facilities and an adult evening institute. The school was founded on an educational philosophy very similar to that of Pestalozzi; both men had been influenced by Rousseau, but Owen's school was not based on Christian principles, as was Pestalozzi's. Robert Owen was an atheist who saw education as an instrument of social change. The school was called 'The Institute for the Formation of Character'. There were no rewards and no punishments; no beatings were allowed, nor were children to be threatened or spoken to abusively. The schoolroom was furnished with paintings, maps and natural objects from the fields and woods which the children were encouraged to examine and discuss. Musical activities were popular and the children had their own band.

Owen believed that the character of children could be moulded in any direction and that correct training would produce rational beings, trained to think of the good of the whole community. He searched out books which would make sense to young children: Robert Dale Owen, Robert Owen's eldest son and collaborator wrote 'The general principle, that children should never be directed to read what they cannot understand, has been found to be of the greatest use'.

In *A New View of Society*, published in 1814, Owen stated:

Reading and writing are merely instruments by which knowledge, either true or false, may be imparted; and when given to children, are of little comparative value, unless they are also taught how to make a proper use of them.

Together with another follower of Pestalozzi, William McLure, Owen later opened a settlement in the United States, called New Harmony, which was short-lived. But his school in New Lanark attracted many visitors and was influential in encouraging the development of infant education in the decades which followed.

Richard and Maria Edgeworth, 1744-1817 and 1767-1849

In Ireland, a schoolmaster by the name of Richard Lovell Edgeworth tried to follow Rousseau's ideas in bringing up his own family. He, his second wife, and his novelist daughter, Maria, carefully recorded their observations of, and conversations with, children. He and his daughter based their educational work and writing upon these observations:

> The first object should not be to teach them reading or grammar, or Latin or arithmetic . . . but gradually to give them the desire to learn and the power to attend . . . they must be taught to think . . . Instead of pressing forward the pupils to astonish parents by the rapidity of their progress, masters should patiently and courageously conquer by delay. They should make the children understand, as much as possible, the reason of all they do. (*Essays on Professional Education*, R.L. Edgeworth)

In Maria Edgeworth's book *Essays on Practical Education*, published in 1815, she writes of the need to integrate the curriculum:

> The persisting to teach things separately, which ought to be taught as a whole, must prevent the progress of mental cultivation. The division and subdivision of different parts of education . . . must tend to increase and perpetuate error.

Yet still in very many schools, the time-table is composed of separate subjects.

Johann Friedrich Herbart, 1776-1841 – using psychology in teaching

One of the lesser-known but nevertheless influential of educators, Herbart was as a young man a tutor to three brothers. He subsequently visited Pestalozzi and taught at his school for a short time and he went on to develop Pestalozzi's ideas for 'psychological education' into a comprehensive theory of learning. As Professor of Philosophy at Königsberg, and later at Göttingen, pedagogics was always an important area of his work. Herbart echoed Quintilian when he wrote, in *The Application of Psychology*, of:

> The dangerous novelty of objects, which heaped up together may later produce an incurable dread of school . . . The danger of arousing fear by the presentation of the new in teaching is specially serious on account of its paralysing effect upon the will.

He showed great insight into the minds of students, describing how we feel when we are confronted by large quantities of factual information, strange to us, and the ways in which pupils may react to having too much pushed at them, too fast. Here he describes two reactions to over-teaching:

> But I have in mind that secret fear which assumes an appearance of indolence and laziness in learning and work, and wherein the mind wanders while the body sits quietly before us. Many are frightened at foreign names, Greek characters, algebraic symbols and geometric figures, who know how to throw a fair enough cloak over the emotion of fear, by asking for congenial intellectual occupations just when efforts are being made to cultivate their minds and taste . . . Such complain that they do not see the 'good' in certain lessons and ask to be allowed to change them, the cause really being that they are afraid of the new symbols. In vigorous natures, instead of this fear, suppressed anger is aroused.

For Herbart, such fear, producing self-doubt and a lack of confidence in one's ability to deal with the new, would be anti-educational and crippling to the development of the child. Thus early education was of great importance; no child should be made to feel inadequate or be discouraged by the thought of future difficulties. The setting of tasks too difficult for a pupil would also cause loss of confidence in the teacher and expose the teacher's ignorance of the needs of the pupil.

What was happening in the mind of the child was of crucial importance:

> How his circle of thought is being formed is everything to the teacher, for out of thoughts come feelings, and from them, principles and modes of action. (*The Science of Education*)

In Herbart's terminology, the circle of thought was formed by thought processes through which new knowledge was absorbed, by association with that already known. He emphasised the concrete, and the need to begin with the pupil's present knowledge before introducing new material. Like Piaget and Bruner in the 20th century he constantly underlined the need to provide children with a wide range of first-hand experience. In *The Science of Education*, he explains his ideas for educating a young child, although, as he admits, he himself had no children:

> I have suggested marking out with bright nails on a board the typical triangles and placing them continually within sight of the child in its cradle. I was laughed at. Well, people may laugh at me still more! For I, in thought, place near the board, sticks and balls painted with various colours; I constantly change, combine and vary these sticks, and later on, plants, and the child's playthings of every kind. I take a little organ into the nursery and sound simple tones and intervals on it for a minute at a time . . . I would further exercise the child's sense to distinguish cold and heat by the thermometer, and to estimate the degrees of heaviness by weights. Finally I would send the child to school with the cloth manufacturer to learn as correctly as he to distinguish finer and coarser wool by touch.

These ideas might have caused laughter in the opening years of the 19th century but they are commonplace in the closing years of the 20th.

Herbart was opposed to large classes because he believed that in order to deal with a throng of students the teacher was forced to develop bureaucratic routines. He saw the role of the teacher as crucial and bent his efforts to making it easier for teachers to understand the ways in which learning took place. He was also concerned to show teachers the pitfalls arising from some of the practices then current.

For Herbart the aim of education was to develop adults of morality and virtue. He saw teachers having an active role in this education, unlike Froebel who encouraged non-intervention on the part of the teacher. The desire of the child for activity and self-development was positive and, with the correct education, the child would readily grow into an adult for whom virtue was an expression of will. For such a person, self-interest would be identical with the interests of society.

Herbart put forward a method which he felt would assist the teacher to present new material in a way which would be more efficient because it was in harmony with the thought processes of the pupil. Unfortunately this work was taken up by doctrinaire followers later in the century and turned into a rigid teaching system which became influential in the United States and in Britain in the early years of this century. His work was vulgarised and became 'The Method', but his name is no longer widely known among educationalists.

Albertine Necker de Saussure, 1765 – 1841

Perhaps the first time that the term 'progressive' was used was when Albertine Necker de Saussure wrote *Progressive Education*, published in France in 1828. Like Herbart she considered the early years of the child, especially the first, a most important period. She studied her own children, and deduced from their development the kind of education which would be most effective; that based on first-hand experience and the child's own desire to master his or her environment. As for school, she criticised the tendency of teachers to teach facts for memorisation, which they could then test:

> As long as instructors attach a higher value to temporary success, than to the motives which prompted the efforts by which that success was obtained – as long as they attend more to external acquisitions than to internal feelings, they will never

succeed in bringing the faculties of the mind to their greatest perfection.

It is true enough that every fresh acquisition of knowledge must add to the cultivation of the faculties; but it is equally true, that our being more occupied in merely storing the mind with information than in the full development of all its powers, is the cause of the greatest part of the defects of instruction.

Friedrich Froebel, 1782-1852 – mystic gardener

Froebel, like Herbart, worked with Pestalozzi. For him too the child's concrete experience should precede words, but unlike Herbart, he was less concerned with investigating how children acquired knowledge, than with allowing their natures to develop freely. He saw education very much in horticultural terms:

> Little children . . . ought not to be *schooled* and taught, they need merely to be *developed*. It is the pressing need of our age, and only the idea of a garden can serve to show us symbolically . . . the proper treatment of children. (*Letters on the Kindergarten*)

And, of course, it was from this belief of his that the word 'kindergarten' or garden of children, has come. His contribution to the progressive tradition is dealt with more fully in Chapter 13.

Putting ideas into practice

In the United States William McLure opened the first Pestalozzian school in Philadelphia in 1809. Others followed: William Woodbridge in New England, Solyman Brown and Henry Barnard; Bronson Alcott, (father of the writer Louisa M. Alcott) opened the Temple Schools for the poor. E.A. Sheldon, working in an Orphan and Free School in Oswego, introduced natural objects as a means of instruction. From this school a movement spread throughout the United States and became known as the Oswego movement. An Herbartian society was set up, and one of its members was John Dewey, who was to develop the idea of progressive, experience-based schools throughout the United States later in the century.

The early 19th century was thus demonstrably a time when hundreds, perhaps thousands of teachers in Great Britain, Europe and North America were moving towards the educational ideas, as old as education itself, which had through the centuries been advocated by those teachers, reformers and philosophers who were part of the developmental tradition. These were not new ideas, but part of educational history. The growth in the numbers of schools at this time, the need for more widespread education, stimulated a new interest in such methods. With the appointment of the earliest Inspectors of Schools, there began to be documentation about the ways in which teachers were actually teaching. There is evidence that there was a variety of methods being used.

A notable village school

The village school at King's Somborne in Hampshire was reported on by one of the first Inspectors, Rev Moseley, in 1847. There science was taught by reference to the children's daily experience; their toys, like squirters, and their knowledge of the village pump grew into lessons on atmospheric pressure; the boiling of water related to steam power, and so on. The curriculum was based on the local environment: considerable time was spent out of doors observing and recording the local flora and fauna, looking for patterns and noting differences. Writing began with what the child knew, the farm animals, crops, events in and features of the locality. There was an aesthetic curriculum in the school and, as HMI pointed out, 'the headmaster's system deals with things rather than words . . . it is for this reason that thinking and doing are associated with pleasurable reactions'. In his judgement the level of the children's attainment was above average in the basic subjects because, rather than in spite of, the broad, integrated and experience-based curriculum available:

> I have certainly never examined little children who could spell so well, and that good spelling and good reading and skill in expression of written thoughts go together may be taken as an illustration of the fact that to achieve excellence in any one subject of instruction in any elementary school it is necessary to unite it with others, and that the singular slowness with which the children of our National Schools learn to read (a fact to which all our reports have borne testimony) is in some degree to be attributed to the unwise concentration of the labours of the school on that single subject.

In 1981 the Department of Education and Science (DES) produced a document, *The School Curriculum*, which had this to say:

> There is no evidence that a narrow curriculum, concentrating only on the basic skills, enables children to do better in these skills: HM Inspectors' survey suggests that competence in reading, writing and mathematics may be improved where pupils are involved in a wider programme of work and if their skills in language and mathematics are applied in a variety of contexts.

There are 134 years between these reports. How is it that so little has been learned, not by the pupils, but by those who make educational policy, the politicians?

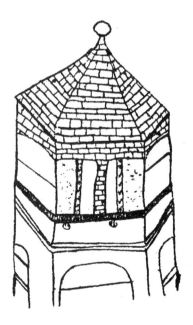

3 | Which tradition are we talking about?

Readers may well wonder why, if a broad and integrated curriculum was found to raise the general level of children's education in 1847, this statement needed to be made again in 1981. This was especially curious since from 1976 onward there had been the exhortation by politicians that schools should get 'back to the basics'. That such a call was made indicated an alarming degree of ignorance on their part. They were not only apparently unaware of the findings of the Inspectorate over previous decades, that schools where there was a broader and more stimulating curriculum achieved greater pupil progress, but they were also ignorant of the extent to which contemporary schools were already concentrating on those basics to the detriment of pupil progress.

This call was linked with a move to demand greater accountability from teachers. What, precisely, did accountability mean? That everything a teacher did had to be weighed in terms of measurable outcomes? Would it be necessary to test every pupil annually to determine whether or not, at the end of a year's teaching, pupils' reading ages had risen by at least one year, mathematical skills and scientific approach ditto? How could areas like social studies be assessed? Even more difficult would be assessment in the whole range of aesthetic education which would involve subjective judgement and a high degree of specialism. What of moral and religious education, how could those be measured? If a pupil had made prodigious progress in the previous year, reached a high plateau in learning, and then appeared to be consolidating, or having a fallow period, progressing less than one year in measurable terms, did this indicate failure on the part of the teacher? Can learning really be assessed in such terms?

When government ministers talk about 'good' teachers being offered rewards, one wonders how 'good' would be determined. Would it be those teachers whose pupils have the best results in measurable areas? And would teachers then be rewarded according to those results? This brings to mind the warning of Madame de Saussure about the dangers of concentrating on visible outcomes rather than on what is going on inside the child.

The Assessment of Performance Unit (APU) was set up by the government in 1975 to provide information on pupils' levels of attainment in single areas of the curriculum, and while it was able to do so in maths and science, many other areas have proved more difficult. The report on language testing has been produced only recently. It was demonstrated once again that too much concentration on those good old-fashioned virtues so much valued by the Victorians, precision and neatness, can be limiting to creativity. The APU publication, *Language Testing 1979-83*, claimed that teachers spent so much time correcting spelling and punctuation and demanding neatness that they encouraged pupils to view writing in too simplified a fashion. But spelling, punctuation and neatness are more easily measured than is creativity.

There have been consistent manifestations during the lifetime of recent administrations of a desire to increase central control of both the curriculum and the purse strings of education. This has been justified by politicians by reference to the *Black Papers*, whose prejudiced and mistaken view of what was happening in primary schools was magnified by the media in the 1960s and 1970s. This was a time of severe teacher shortage, over-sized classes and part-time schooling. The Prime Minister, James Callaghan, intervened in 1976 to initiate 'The Great Debate'. The Secretary of State for Education, Shirley Williams, took part in meetings with parents, teachers and other interested groups, in various parts of the country, and in the following year the DES published a Green Paper, *Education in Schools: a Consultative Document*, which stated some general aims and put considerable emphasis on the need to teach basic skills. In this document Mr Callaghan stated that he was inclined to think that there should be a basic curriculum with universal standards, i.e. more centralisation. He also made it clear that there could be little expectation of further resources being made available to education. More recently, Education Secretaries Sir Keith Joseph and Kenneth Baker have echoed these calls for a central curriculum and Baker has said he wants to set objectives for what children should be learning at ages seven, nine, and 11.

Such statements by leading politicians, who call for higher standards but are unwilling to resource the steps which would bring them about, sound alarming to teachers and should alarm parents likewise. Rumours of centrally drawn-up syllabi to be used in all schools, together with annual measurement of teaching outcomes, put one in mind of the 'payment by results' period, so it may be salutary to consider its effects.

Payment by results

In 1858 the Newcastle Commission was appointed. Its terms of reference:

> To inquire into the present state of popular education in England, and to consider and report what measures, if any, are required for the extension of sound and cheap elementary instruction to all classes of the people.

The Commission found that educational standards were very low generally. Their findings echoed those of Rev Moseley a decade earlier. It found that:

> A large proportion of the children are not satisfactorily taught that which they come to school to learn . . . A large proportion of them . . . in some districts do not learn even to read; at least their power of reading is so slight, so little connected with any intelligent perception of its importance, and so much a matter of mere mechanical routine, as to be of little value to them in after-life, and to be frequently forgotten as soon as the school is left . . . They neither read well nor write well. They work sums, but they learn their arithmetic in such a way as to be of little practical use in common life.

The solution proposed was that every child should be examined annually by an Inspector. Instead of payments being made direct to certificated teachers they were from then on to be made to school managers who could claim specified amounts for pupils of different ages, according to their attendance at school, *subject to their satisfactory examination*. Out of these grants the managers would pay the teachers and equip the schools. When this Revised Code was introduced in 1862, Robert Lowe, Vice-President of the Privy Council Committee on Education, told the House of Commons:

I cannot promise the House that this system will be an economical one and I cannot promise that it will be an efficient one, but I can promise that it shall be one or the other. If it is not cheap it shall be efficient; if it is not efficient it shall be cheap.

Precise and detailed tests were set out in six standards. This was effectively a centrally-controlled curriculum because, although there was no prohibition on the teaching of other subjects there was a tremendous pressure on teachers to spend all their time preparing pupils for these examinations and ensuring that they were word perfect. The system was known as 'payment by results' and certainly lowered government spending on education (from £813,441 in 1861 to £636,806 by 1865) which was no doubt a cause for congratulation in some circles. It could in no way be deemed efficient. To quote from *The Struggle for Education*, published by the National Union of Teachers in 1970:

Among particular grievances were the 'music fine' – for anything taught outside the six standards represented a loss for the school managers – and the principle of grouping by age. Brighter children were held back and dull ones were coerced in order to reach the required levels. Endless drilling of young children, liberally supported by corporal punishment, was therefore imposed on the schools in those crucial decades . . . Because of the desperate importance of satisfying the inspectors – and up to two-thirds of a school's grant depended on these exams, teachers became accomplices in innumerable tricks and dodges. They would inform each other of the habits of particular inspectors, convey information to their children by signs like a card sharper, force those who could not read to memorise relevant passages and avoid taking in children who were likely to fail to reach the necessary standards.

A poignant extract from a school log book in 1871 is quoted by Gordon & Lawton in their book, *Curriculum Change in the 19th and 20th Centuries*. It was written by the headmaster of a Welsh school:

Believing that one-fourth of the school time that was devoted to subjects not recognised by government, and consequently not paid for by grants, had the effect of keeping a well-informed school but of causing the percentage results to be lower than those of the schools that are mechanical in their working and unintelligible in their tone, I have been compelled against my inclination to arrange that less time be devoted to them in future and more time to those that pay best.

Thus, under the 'payment by results' system 'well-informed' pupils became less desirable than those drilled mechanically and unintelligibly. But central control of the purse strings of education left teachers without choice. The curriculum had to be narrowed to those areas most easily tested speedily, involving the kind of chicanery described above. Could anything be further from positive and useful education?

The system of 'payment by results' was gradually eroded over the years but was not to be finally eradicated until the 1890s, although it was as early as 1867 when Matthew Arnold, the poet and critic, who for 26 years was an Inspector of Schools, reported that:

The mode of teaching in the primary schools has certainly fallen off in intelligence, spirit and inventiveness during the four or five years which have elapsed since my last report. It could not well be otherwise. In a country where everyone is prone to rely too much on mechanical processes and too little on intelligence, a change in the Education Department's regulations, which, by making two-thirds of the government grant depend upon a mechanical examination, inevitably gives a mechanical turn to the school teaching, a mechanical turn to the inspection, is, and must be, trying to the intellectual life of a school . . .

The idea of payment by results was just the idea to be caught up by the ordinary public opinion of this country and to find favour with it . . . and is likely to be pressed by it to further applications. But the question is not whether this idea, or this or that application of it suits ordinary public opinion and school managers; the question is whether it really suits the interests of the schools and their instruction. In this country we are somewhat unduly liable to regard the latter suitableness too little and the former too much. I feel sure from my experience of foreign schools as well as of our own, that our present system of grants does harm to schools and their instruction by resting its grants

too exclusively, at any rate, upon individual examination, pre-
scribed in all its details beforehand by the Central Office.

Would more central control improve education?

Clearly any attempt to reintroduce this kind of central control into
British education must be viewed with great suspicion by teachers
and parents alike, especially since the government's anxiety to
reduce spending on education, like that of the government of 1862,
has already resulted in lower spending and greater inefficiency.
This is made clear in the most recent Report by HMI on *The
Effects of Local Authority Expenditure Policies on Education
Provision in England* in 1985, which stated:

> Many pupils and teachers are having to work in accommodation
> which is inappropriate and does not offer a civilized environment
> . . . Few involved in providing or providing for education can
> take much, if any, pride in a national service within which three-
> tenths of all the lessons seen were unsatisfactory; one-fifth was
> adversely affected by poor accommodation; a quarter was suffer-
> ing from shortages of equipment; in three-fifths of the schools
> where an assessment was possible, the teachers' perceptions
> of pupils' potential and needs were inadequate; and half the
> schools visited needed to widen their range of teaching styles
> to bring about a better match with what was taught.

Like so many previous HMI Reports this is an indictment of
government policies because however much responsibility falls on
the local education authorities (and there is a great gap between
the best providers and the worst) the poorest providers are those
who have been encouraged by government policies to cut down
on spending. On the other hand the Inner London Education
Authority (ILEA), which is responsible for those who live in areas
of urban decay, suffering many forms of deprivation, has been
under constant attack from the government for over-spending. So
too, criticisms of teachers have to be seen in the context of years
of being undervalued, and of their campaign for salaries which
reflect a recognition of the kind of commitment in time and effort
made by the majority of teachers.

Further, if as claimed by HMI, some teachers are sticking too
rigidly to too narrow a range of methods and are nervous about
experimenting with a wider range, who can blame them after all

the exhortations to return to so-called 'traditional methods' and to concentrate on the basics, which they have heard from government sources. As well as which, of course, they are constricted in many cases by too-large classes working in poor accommodation and lack the equipment needed to develop their work in the way HMI would like to see.

It is worthy of note that the Audit Commission (itself set up by the government) in its 1986 report 'came down strongly against centralisation towards which the present Department of Education has shown signs of moving'. (*The Guardian* 15 May 1986) If even the auditors can recognise the dangers of increasing centralisation – which means giving most power to those who know least about education – surely parents and teachers can combine to prevent this.

What do they mean by 'falling standards'?

> Lord Young, the Employment Secretary, said yesterday that educational standards were falling and must be raised as a matter of urgency. (*The Guardian* 12 May 1986)

I have often wondered precisely *when* was the golden age of education. We know from the quotations above that it was not 1847, nor 1858, nor the decades which followed. In *Black Paper Two* (Cox and Dyson), Cyril Burt wrote: 'Judged by tests applied and standardised in 1913-14, the average attainments in reading, spelling, mechanical and problem arithmetic are now appreciably lower than they were 55 years ago'. Thus, since he was writing in 1969, it would seem that Professor Burt considered the first one-and-a-half decades of the century to have been an educational high point. Yet in 1912 a conference of the English Association was told by a training college lecturer:

> It is a fact that the average boy and girl on leaving school are unable to write English with clearness and fluency or with any degree of grammatical accuracy. (*The Times* 15 January 1912)

A statement which casts some doubt upon Professor Burt's conclusion.

In 1925 a Report by HMI announced:

> From the best in reading aloud (for 12-year-olds) it appeared

that in many schools children reach this stage without having mastered the mechanical difficulties of reading. (*Annual Report on the Teaching of English in London Elementary Schools*)

In 1938 came the Spens Report, *Secondary Education with Special Reference to Grammar Schools and Technical High Schools*:

> It is a common and grave criticism that many pupils pass through the *grammar schools (and even through the universities)* without acquiring the capacity to express themselves in English. [My emphasis]

The same complaints were made about arithmetic standards:

> Accuracy in the manipulation of figures does not reach the same standard which was reached 20 years ago. (*The Teaching of Arithmetic in Elementary Schools*, 1925)

Both World Wars revealed alarming illiteracy among recruits to the armed forces. In 1941 there was public consternation when it was realised how low were the reading standards of many conscripts. It was this concern and a determination to provide a more equal and efficient education service which led finally to the 1944 Education Act. And Professor Burt, who made such sweeping accusations about low standards in British schools in the 1960s, wrote an article on adult illiteracy in *The British Journal of Educational Psychology* in 1945:

> Recent surveys have shown that the amount of illiteracy among adults in this country is unexpectedly large, and provides a pressing problem for the educationist. Taking the borderlines for illiteracy and semi-illiteracy as indicated by reading ages of about six-and-a-half and eight years respectively, it would appear that by the age of about 21 one-and-a-half to two per cent of the population are illiterate and 15 to 20 per cent semi-literate.

The adults in the surveys referred to by Professor Burt would of course have been educated during the previous 50 years, which rather discounts his later criticisms of educational standards as being lower in 1969 than they were in 1914. It is also worthy of note that much of Professor Burt's work has now been discredited, first by Professor Leon Kamin, of Princeton University, with his findings being later endorsed by other researchers at Hull University. Yet his ideas were most influential in shaping the old tri-partite secondary educational system in Britain. He is also much quoted by those who claim that standards are falling, in spite of the disrepute into which his work has fallen.

If standards aren't falling, are our expectations rising?

A very different view on educational progress was given in the Newsome Report, *Half Our Future*, 1963, which noted:

> Another fact, perhaps not often enough emphasised is that the standard indicated by 'average' is rising all the time, perhaps never more rapidly than in the last 25 years . . . In . . . a series of tests designed to show the pupils' capacity to read with understanding, there is a clear record of improvement. A test score which even 14 years ago would have been enough to put boys and girls well into the above-average category would today put them firmly into the below-average group. Over the intervening years the general level of performance has risen . . .

> One of the reasons why there is a quite proper anxiety over the general standards of literacy today is not that fewer and fewer people can read and write but that more and more people need to do so with greater competence.

Fourteen years later, in 1977, an inspection of 542 schools, involving 1,127 classes, was undertaken by HM Inspectors. They examined the work being done by pupils of seven, nine and 11 years. Their report, *Primary Education in England*, found that there had been an improvement in the reading of children at the age of 11, as shown by their scoring system:

	1955	1966	1970	1976/7
Mean score	28.70	29.47	29.38	31.13

And, interestingly enough, the APU Language Survey, 1986 says that 'contrary to public opinion' only about 3 per cent of pupils 'have great difficulty with writing'.

It is also instructive to note that, as reported in *The Independent* (8 January 1987), a recent DES survey showed that earlier figures suggesting a decline in the proportion of young people obtaining A levels had been based on misleading data. When A level students at further education colleges were taken into account, the proportion of 17-year-olds who obtained at least one A level was shown to have risen steadily since 1971.

While I would not, in any way, suggest that there is ground for complacency in these statistics, I do not think the case for raising educational levels is enhanced by the kind of alarmism that breaks out regularly in the media. If our expectations are rising, (and they *should* rise – we *should* expect progress in education), then we have to be conscious that this is so and not hark back to a non-existent Golden Age in which brilliant (though underpaid) teachers consistently produced whole classes of young geniuses. Instead we have to examine carefully those steps in the past which brought about improvements in education, and avoid those which caused deterioration. It is clear from the evidence above that 'payment by results' was a disaster for education in the 19th century and there seems little likelihood of it producing any improvements in this one.

If, as all the various HMI reports indicate, a broad and integrated curriculum is advantageous at primary stage, then surely it is time to stop calling for returns to the 'basics'. This has in the past led to a dull, mechanical and repetitive curriculum under which pupils were unable to develop their potential and did not lead to their acquisition of even those elementary skills on which the curriculum was concentrated. Perhaps governments need to be reminded of Robert Lowe's inability to provide a system that was both efficient and cheap. The cheap system turned out to be extremely expensive in terms of lack of educational achievement and the waste of resources that implied. The dilemma of governments seems to be how to provide for the educational advance we all expect *without* the requisite expenditure. A whole range of cliches could be used to describe the situation from 'spoiling the ship for a ha'p'orth of tar', to 'you get what you pay for'.

The human cost of returning to Victorian values

All the solutions which have come from various government sources have in some way involved the reintroduction of the discarded selection principle, which would mean that the selected few would get a decent education, while the many would once again be robbed of the opportunity to develop their potential. We must not forget all the evidence of the recent past which showed the waste of talent that took place because selection at 11-plus was so inefficient, even in its own terms, that many children of high intelligence did not pass the test, while others who did pass had, in fact, less possibility of making the best of what they were offered in the grammar schools. We have heard about voucher schemes, industrial funding of schools, and so on: all of them devices to solve the problem of educational provision on the cheap, and all of them doomed to failure.

They are doomed to failure because it is not possible to provide an education system which offers the fullest opportunities to all pupils without proper financing. The option of fee-paying education presupposes that schools in the private sector are necessarily superior to those in the public sector, which is simply not true, although many have the advantage of smaller class size. It also avoids the issue that Britain needs *all* its youngsters educated well so that future generations do not grow up with the bitter knowledge of wasted years and unrealised potential. We are constantly being told that we are falling behind technologically: to remedy that we must give all pupils the opportunities to develop the understanding and skills required.

When we hear traditional values being invoked we should ask 'Which tradition?' Are we speaking of the tradition developed in schools such as Robert Owen's, King's Somborne and others before 1862, or is it the tradition of schools during the period of the Revised Code, with the dead hand of the 'payment by results' system upon them? The first tradition would enable us to make the kind of progress in education which is necessary. The second tradition would once again close doors to any real educational advance.

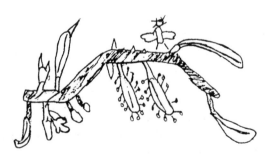

4 | Getting down to the basics

What exactly is meant when calls are made to go 'back to the basics'? In my childhood the phrase 'the three Rs' was popular. Presumably this referred to Reading, 'Riting and 'Rithmetic! The basics are normally seen as being literacy and numeracy, and there are those who think that constant exercises in those areas will produce higher standards. Education for them consists of memorising facts and methods and practising these thoroughly. Sometimes these views are combined with a wish to 'cut out the frills' which are seen as a waste of public money. It is unarguable that literacy and numeracy are two of the expected outcomes of primary education, but so is oracy (a word coined recently in educational circles to represent the range of speech skills), and so is a wide experience of the whole field of aesthetic education desirable. Yet there are many areas of the country now where children only have access to playing a musical instrument if their parents can afford to pay for lessons. There are also schools where the cost of paints and clay and sewing and modelling materials is increasingly beyond the school budget. There has been a decline in the amount of money spent by schools on books. Could it be that the desire to limit education to literacy and numeracy is as much concerned with economy as with improving educational levels in those areas of the curriculum?

Education for what?

Before we can decide on what is the most desirable form of education, perhaps we should consider the purpose of education. Why do we have to send our children to school, or at least satisfy the local education authority that we are educating them adequately at home, if we so choose? We have to send our children to school, between the ages of five and 16, because this is the law. I have no doubt that if a referendum were held, in this or any other country, on the desirability of children being compelled to attend school, there would be a vast majority in favour. One of the characteristics of developing countries is the immense value placed on education, and the efforts made to provide education for all is regarded as an index of good government. If we want to improve the quality of life for our children and generations to come, then we have the responsibility of enabling them to understand and learn to control the physical world in which they live, and to communicate fully in as many modes as possible – to enjoy the physical and aesthetic world, to be creative and purposeful and able to enjoy the creativity of others, to have self-respect and to respect others.

There will be differences between cultures and individuals: some parents want their children to grow up within a religious faith, others might have particular ambitions in terms of future employment, but by and large we all, parents and teachers, want to see children develop their full potential. The organisation of our school system has developed partly to meet this wish, but partly for other reasons.

Centuries ago, most children learned at home, and what they learned was limited by the kind of home in which they lived. Thus the children of weavers would learn to weave and the children of farmers would learn to farm. While not all children followed their parents' occupation, this was the general pattern. Sometimes children learned to read and write – many large villages had schools and market towns usually had a free grammar school, but there was no compulsion to attend. Well-to-do families would have tutors; young children and girls were often taught by their mothers. There were schools which catered for a minority of boys and which formed the nucleus of the public school system. At the other end of the social scale there were the thousands of paupers in work-houses and orphanages.

The Industrial Revolution, by establishing factories which took mothers and fathers out of the home, made it more difficult for them to combine earning a living with child care. Very young children worked in the factories, before the Factory Acts of the early 19th century ended this practice. I have already referred to Robert Owen and the school he founded at his New Lanark mill. Children remained there until the age of ten; then, old enough for employment, their education continued after work only, although Robert Owen and his son would have preferred the pupils to stay longer at school. Other infant schools were founded, many by

Samuel Wilderspin. He had been the master of an infant school in Spitalfields, who then became a crusader for the London Infant School Society and toured the country promoting infant education during the mid-19th century.

The infant school movement, combined with the horror felt at the working conditions of children like the four-year-old climbing boy sweeps and other factory workers of tender years, encouraged the growth of elementary education. The churches became concerned and began to build schools – they also saw these as a means of building their congregations. Another form of care, child-minding rather than education, was provided by the dame schools, in which women, unable through disability or age to get other work, would engage to look after as many local children as possible, for a small fee, while mothers were at work. Some of the women might have been kind and done their best; others undoubtedly were cruel and irresponsible.

So the spread of schools during the 19th century was linked with the need for workers in the growing number of mills and factories where men and women worked 14 or more hours daily for six days of the week. They were obviously maintained as cheaply as possible, often catering for hundreds of children, all together in one large schoolroom. There would be a master in charge, but groups were taught by monitors, who were the oldest children, aged nine or ten, who passed on the skills they had learned: all was done by rote.

As technology advanced, a demand developed for more highly-skilled workers and for clerical workers who could write letters to clients, keep accounts and write out invoices. This led to pressure from factory owners and businessmen for a national school system to train workers for such concerns. Many of the MPs themselves had business interests. And so the Education Act of 1870 called for the building of new schools where necessary in order that the entire child population might be schooled, and the 1880 Act introduced universal and compulsory education. But the aims of this education were that children should grow up with the right moral and religious beliefs, should know their place, and should be educated to be useful in the developing industrial, commercial and colonial empires. In 1881 the Samuelson Commission was set up and its terms of reference were:

To enquire into the instruction of the industrial classes of certain foreign countries in technical and other subjects for the purposes of comparison with that of the corresponding classes in this country; and into the influence of such instruction on manufacturing and other industries at home and abroad.

This demonstrates the direct link between the needs of manufacturing industry and the developing curriculum in the schools. Whether or not the school curiculum should still be so determined is debatable.

However, the Commission did not find the curriculum adequate: even from a utilitarian point of view, the basic skills were not enough. It called for the introduction of drawing, more object lessons, more craft work and agriculture, thus indicating that even when the aim is to develop the basic skills, a wider curriculum than literacy and numeracy is desirable. So yet again, in 1882 a narrow curriculum is found to be inadequate.

Learning the basics

A broad curriculum is not only desirable but essential because children do not learn by having facts hammered into them. Most rote learning, unless accompanied by understanding, does not remain in the memory. To be retained, learning must be understood, and skills practised in a variety of ways. Learning the basics – acquiring the basic skills of speaking, reading, writing and counting – requires a wide range of applications in different situations before the learner can become competent. And since we no longer hold that children should be educated only to fit them for employment and keep them moral, we must add the aims of acquainting children with their human cultural heritage, ensuring their physical, aesthetic and moral development, and providing them with opportunities to make choices so that they can learn to profit from their mistakes and make wise decisions.

Children also need to learn *how* to learn and how to continue to learn, because education is not synonymous with schooling. Children begin to learn from the moment they are born and a very important part of their education takes place at home. People go on learning for as long as they live and research has shown that the more that new learning takes place as one gets older, the less the brain deteriorates.

Education is a continuous process, but different ways of learning are appropriate at different stages of development. In our society we have, for convenience, organised the school system in some areas into Nursery (3-5), Infant (5-7) and Junior (7-11), or Primary (5-11), and Secondary (11-18). In other parts of the country there are Middle Schools (8-12 or 9-13) or Lower and Upper Secondary Schools, but these are very rough stages and no-one believes that each child at five, seven, nine or 11 has reached precisely the same level as all his or her peers. There can be as great a variation between children in the same school year as there is between one year group and another. Since we begin the school year officially on September 1st of each year, the child born on that day, although only one day younger than the child born on 31st August, is officially in the previous school age group, and is practically a whole year older than the child born in August of the same school year as himself. Rates of progress also vary between child and child, and for the same child at different times.

Oracy – learning to speak

Adults, and children too, are fascinated when babies begin to imitate speech. First words are celebrated and much time is spent encouraging the beginnings of speech. The baby takes its cue from those surrounding it and responds to smiles and cuddles by making more rewarding sounds. Soon the baby discovers that certain words have the power to bring about desirable ends – food, drink, or a wanted toy. Gradually the baby is transformed into a prattling toddler and then reaches a stage where its speech is no longer so welcomed. The stream of questions, the 'why' stage sometimes irritates a tired parent, and the child's speech may become inhibited through fear of parental antagonism. In a large family the young child might have to fight for a share of parental time, but a compensation would be conversations with siblings. In a small one, parents might have more time to speak to the child, but unless there are plenty of opportunities to play with other children, the child might miss out on conversations with his or her peers. Many people still believe that children should be seen but not heard and try to prevent children from joining in general conversation.

When the child begins school much will depend upon the kind of expectations there. The child going into a nursery or infant class where there is lots of conversation with children and where children are listened to, will be encouraged to speak more, leading to a greater development of language. But in all too many schools the command 'Stop talking' is still heard. Of course there are times when silence is necessary – when a class is listening to others or during an assembly – but when children are working in class, discussion is often helpful. Sometimes when a mechanical task is being carried out adults also like to chat to one another, so why not children? How can children develop their use of spoken language unless they do talk – and listen, and are listened to by others? This allowance of talking time in school is very important – children need to learn to discuss, debate and argue. They need to listen to the arguments of others, reflect and come to new conclusions. They need an arena in which to test their opinions and observations in speech.

We would do well to remember Pestalozzi's injunction, not so much to talk *to* a child but to enter into conversation *with* a child. Comenius placed importance upon the early development of speech and advised mothers to bring objects to their children and name them. He suggested that anything remarked on by a child, during a walk, for instance, should be discussed by parent and child and should also be drawn by the child at home. And other educators of the past believed that children learned by doing, and would learn to speak best by speaking and through direct experience. In the first chapter I referred to the old controversy about teaching by rule. It is instructive to reflect that young children do not learn to speak by being taught rules, but by copying the speech patterns they hear, repeating them and attempting to generalise from their experience. That is why so many small children, having learned that the addition of 's' forms a plural will add it, very logically, where the plural is irregular, to 'sheep' for example. Adults on hearing a small child say 'A lot of sheeps' may find this amusing and laugh, correcting the child, but it is the child who is showing intelligence, predicting the common plural, and the adult who is foolish to laugh instead of congratulating the child.

In Hezekiah Woodward's *A Light to Grammar*, written in 1641, he considered that, in speaking, a child already showed knowledge of grammatical structures which eliminated any need for formal teaching:

If grammar can go into the child at the gates of the senses, all science will follow by the same light and at the same door.

This still holds good today for the education of young children.

Literacy – reading and writing

Reading a teacher's notebook recently I noticed a comment about a five-year-old who had not been able to write for herself until one Mothers' Day. Making a Mothers' Day card and writing it herself had been her motivation, and the beginning of her developing writing skills.

The start of reading and writing lies in the interests of the child, and this is what teachers use to motivate pupils. Of course many children have already begun the process before they come to school. They might have been recognising words on cornflakes packets, the name of the road in which they live – they are on the verge of reading. When they are being read to, they will point out particular words which they know, they will remark on words beginning with the initial letter of their own name, and so on. The child who is used to books at home, who has been taken to the public library, who is read to regularly by adults and older children is usually motivated. Sometimes a physical problem intervenes – it may be sight- or hearing-related – but for most children reading skills develop relatively painlessly.

Many teachers now believe that the breaking down of reading into stages could be making learning to read more, rather than less, difficult for children. This means that instead of concentrating on the sounds made by letters before children begin to look at books, or learning a set of words which are then read over and over again in very simple reading books of the 'Look, John, look' variety, children should have interesting books read to them, and be given those books to ponder over the words, and become used to written language. The language in early reading books ought to be more like everyday speech and the books so attractive and interesting that children will want to handle and read them. The distinction between 'reading books' and just books, is becoming blurred. It is no longer thought helpful to correct every word read by a child. Nor to insist that books are read and reread until the child is word perfect. Instead teachers are concerned that the child should understand and enjoy the reading matter. For if we examine the way in which we, as adults, read, we will find that when we come upon a word we do not immediately recognise, we can often work out its meaning from the context. We also skim and skip over words because we are continually predicting what will come next. Reading each word makes reading very laborious and probably turns many children away from an interest in books.

This does mean throwing away all those reading schemes which are boring, repetitive and unattractive, and which contribute nothing to a child's enthusiasm for reading. It also means providing a wide range of books of different degrees of difficulty, so that each child has plenty of opportunity to read at his or her own level. The teacher needs to know the level of all the books and be able to group them so that children can choose from within the group suitable for them at any particular time. It is most important that children approach reading with confidence, feel they can make mistakes without constant interruption bringing the sense of failure which we all feel when we are corrected too often. If we have the patience when listening to children reading, we will find that after making a mistake they will often go back and correct themselves. In reading, as in speech, children constantly endeavour to generalise from their previous experience about the printed word.

Some children need more time, and perhaps more help. The kind of help needed can only be determined by careful observation of children and listening to their reading. Sometimes diagnostic tests will be needed to find out if there are physical causes or if the child has a specific reading difficulty. When the cause of the hold-up is discovered, then particular remedial programmes can be carried out, often by teachers with special training in this field.

Most criticism of reading teaching in schools comes not because the basics are not being taught, but because they are *too* basic. The HMI report *Primary Education in England* (1978) states:

> It was evident that teachers devoted considerable attention to ensuring that children mastered the basic techniques of reading but there was a tendency at all ages for children to receive insufficient encouragement to extend the range of their reading.

In most cases it is the advanced reading skills which are not being learned.

Some children begin to read before they begin to write. Others may be able to write their names, or just groups of letters, before they start to read. For many, their own writing is the best first reading. The beginnings of writing have three roots. One is the physical ability to hold a pencil and make the letters with it, another is being able to put the letters into the right order to make desired words, and the third is actually wanting to communicate those words in a written form. The little girl writing the Mothers' Day card managed to get all three together. Not every five-year-old does, but of those who do, most are girls. Boys often take a little longer.

A teaching aid like *Breakthrough to Literacy* (a scheme devised by David Mackay) is most valuable when a child wants to communicate but has not fully developed the necessary skills, and could be held back in expression because of physical clumsiness in writing or confusion about the constitution of sentences. The physical act of writing is helped considerably by plenty of drawing and painting. The ability to sort out the letters comes gradually, and again confidence is all important. The child who has had plenty of opportunity to speak and get used to patterns of the language, understands sentence structure and has a good vocabulary, will have an advantage. The child whose early efforts are greeted by laughter can become reluctant to risk ridicule and may grow up into the nine-year-old who claims not to want to read or write. What is often meant is that he or she is afraid to make mistakes and be made to feel stupid.

Numeracy − counting or mathematics

Numeracy also begins early, counting stairs or strawberries; helping to lay a table; matching socks and shoes; knowing one has two eyes and two ears but only one nose and mouth; counting fingers, toes and pennies. One thing is very clear to anyone who has observed young children: questions in the abstract have little or no meaning for them. Two and two do not make anything for most young children. But counting two bricks and then another two will frequently bring forth the answer 'four bricks'. It takes time and a lot of experience of the *quantity* four in many varied situations for the child to begin to generalise from that experience and develop the *concept* of four.

Learning to sort things into sets − classifying − is the beginning of mathematics and logic too, and for this laying tables or matching pairs of clothing items provide valuable experience. Learning to recognise differences and similarities, comparisons, measuring and weighing, all help to develop children's understanding of mathematics. For mathematics is much more than counting. When children learn the number symbols and spend most of their time writing these down in different arrangements they are dealing with only a small area of arithmetic – doing 'sums'. If we want children to be able to communicate in the language of mathematics, for it is a language which uses symbols instead of letters, then early mathematical activity needs to be very practical and to provide, once again, a wide range of experience from which children can begin to make mathematical generalisations. Perhaps the emphasis still placed upon getting sums right in our schools derives from the Victorians' need for accurate book-keepers. If we now need more mathematicians then the basic skill of counting, or knowing tables by rote, is not going to be enough. Because of the many controversies about 'modern' mathematics, I will deal with this at greater length in a later chapter.

There really is no question but that the basics *are* being taught in the vast majority of schools. The foreword to the HMI report of 1978 had this to say:

> What emerges from the report is that teachers in primary schools work hard to make pupils well behaved, literate and numerate.

What then can be the cause of this constant emphasis on the need for an education which concentrates on the basics, when these are precisely what are being taught – and learned – to the detriment of the broader education, which most people with educational experience feel is more useful as well as being more desirable? Perhaps, as concentration on the basics fits in with the philosophy that demands that education cost as little as possible, it also fits the desires of those who see education merely as fitting the majority of youngsters for future employment, not now in factories and mills but in a fast-food economy where higher-level skills are unnecessary, and where too much emphasis on thinking for oneself and challenging accepted orthodoxies would be too threatening to the status quo.

The question remains, not only for parents and teachers, but for society, can a basic education, involving the lowest possible expenditure and the acquisition of only the basic skills be the best preparation for life for children who will be living and working in the 21st century?

5 | If it's not what you do, is it the way that you do it?

The common distinction between traditional and progressive, or formal and informal, schools is not particularly helpful because simple homogeneity is not often found. In the course of work I have done – as an examiner of education students hoping to teach younger children, and more recently working on induction programmes for probationary teachers – I have been fortunate enough to visit a large number of primary schools. No two classrooms are ever exactly alike; even in a school where there is strong central leadership from the headteacher and a unified policy, differences will be obvious. In a school where such leadership is not supplied, either for philosophical reasons, or by omission, differences between classes can be very wide indeed. Even a school which has a central policy favouring formality may have one or two informal classrooms which stand out as different from the mainstream, while in a largely informal school there may often be found the formal classroom co-existing. Most schools contain teachers with different, and sometimes conflicting, ideas. It is only rarely that a headteacher has drawn together an entire staff with a common philosophy, although this can happen where the headteacher remains at a school for a long time and those staff who disagreed with the authorised outlook have retired or moved to more congenial schools, and been replaced by others who the headteacher and governors feel will fit in better.

Teachers, like people in other jobs, will vary in their efficiency – just as genius has been said to be a capacity for taking pains, so most good teachers are meticulous organisers. Going out for the day with a class of infants, only to discover that their lunches have been left behind would be a disaster indeed. So would a trip to a theatre, only to find you had arrived on the wrong day. If this happens to a family, disappointment can be soothed by other distractions, but it is quite a different matter when the disappointed number 30 or more!

Classrooms too have to be carefully organised so that everything the children will need to complete their tasks is available to them. While the odd piece of equipment could be borrowed from another class, colleagues would not be very happy to have a constant stream of children arriving at intervals because their class teacher had not been able to organise them earlier. The inability to organise adequately is probably the greatest cause of failure among young teachers. Luckily, most learn this fairly quickly.

Organisation is particularly important with informal teaching. It is often said that such teaching can be successfully carried out by very good teachers, but if teachers are weak then it is best for them to teach formally. While it is probably true that a formal classroom is less likely to become as chaotic as a badly- or unorganised informal room, weak teachers would not be any more inspiring in a formal situation; their pupils would hardly be inflamed with a desire to learn. In fact they may become bored and apathetic and lose all interest in learning.

Most teachers are interested in teaching well and are committed to the children they teach. But young teachers faced with large numbers of children and without the equipment to provide adequate first-hand experience for the class might well be forced into teaching more formally than they would wish, simply because the school they are in is not resourced for them to work in any other way. In such cases, if the teacher remains and retains a belief in the importance of first-hand experiences, rather than taking the easy way out and following the school pattern, he or she might be able to gather up the necessary equipment, work in a different way, and even exert an influence on the curriculum of the school.

There are ways of teaching which are regarded as either traditional or progressive, but when these styles or forms of organisation are looked at more closely the divisions are not always so clear cut. Whether the curriculum being presented to children is one which genuinely facilitates their intellectual and emotional development, or whether they are following instructions only, is determined by much more than their teacher's choice of intended teaching style.

Teaching a class as individuals

What complicates any analysis of teaching styles is that teachers can be found teaching in a way which is regarded as 'progressive' because it is individual, while the children's curriculum is entirely based on textbooks or work sheets. I have found this situation in some schools which look very modern, especially those which are open-plan and where economy has dictated minimal space and maximum class size. I remember visiting one such school in lovely rural surroundings, some years ago. Class base areas were separated from one another only by low storage units and it was possible for a standing adult to survey the whole school. There were many pleasant features; the school was fully carpeted – children were required to bring soft shoes or slippers for indoor wear. There was a small room for music, another for cookery, two bays for painting and craftwork, and a hall for PE and school meals. The atmosphere was hushed and orderly. Some children were queueing at their teachers' desks, others were busily writing but there was no practical work of any kind to be seen. When I asked the headteacher about this he explained that lack of space and the need to keep a low noise level because of the acoustics of the building meant that movement and sound were kept to a mimimum and children worked quietly from textbooks or work sheets. They took their completed work up to their teacher for marking and if their work was satisfactory they would be presented with their next task. Story reading was synchronised throughout the school for the same reason. Children took turns to use the painting space: each child got a turn in the art room for about 20 minutes each week – everything had to be rigidly time-tabled. He was not very happy with the arrangement, but felt that the school's saving grace was the rural environment for it meant teachers could take their classes outside to work whenever the weather allowed.

In that school there was individual work being carried out, but the curriculum offered to the pupils was extremely formal and there was an absence of co-operative work and discussion by the children. They did not have opportunities for experiment, nor for arguing and developing lines of reasoning. There was little opportunity for them to learn how to make choices. Nor did the teachers have time to talk to the children about their work because they were fully occupied in occupying the pupils and keeping the noise level down. The longer the queues waiting for the teacher, the faster the teacher needed to mark, the less time there was for discussion of a mistake. If an idea needed correcting, there was no time for a dialogue in which the pupil could be brought to see the error for him or herself; instead the teacher had to tell the child what was wrong, a far less efficient way of teaching. From observation, many children I have seen working this way are thoroughly bored; most will be obedient and try to please, but this is not what education should be about.

Thus a school with superficially progressive characteristics was forced by physical constraints to work in a most formal way.

Teaching as telling

The didactic teacher is one who *tells* the class what he or she considers relevant and sets them appropriate tasks. This style of teaching is also known as 'chalk and talk' because of the heavy use of the blackboard. It is usually combined with whole-class teaching and the same task may be set for every child. It is the easiest way of working with an over-large class, and is therefore popular with those responsible for allocating finance to education. When practical work is done, it is often done by the teacher, demonstrating to the class, or to groups, while the children, having watched the demonstration, then write notes, often based on the answers to questions written on the blackboard or merely copy the notes already written up by the teacher. On looking through such children's work, a remarkable uniformity may be found. Very little is demanded from the pupil in the way of initiative or independent thought; in fact this might be penalised and equated with disobedience because the ideas developed in such a class are those of the teacher and not those of the child. Here, a good memory, the ability to regurgitate received information and conformity are prized attributes.

I once saw didactic teaching taken to an extreme degree, with six-year-olds, in a manner that seemed ridiculous and even tragic to me and my companions. Four of us, qualified teachers, were on a visit to an infant school in a new building, in a delightful, landscaped setting. When we arrived we were met by the headmistress who told us something of the history and sociology of the school. She told us also that the children were very difficult and there was a particular problem with enuretic children. Each year, she said, there seemed to be more and more children who wet their pants in school.

We were then taken to a classroom where 30 or more small children were sitting at rows of tables, all facing the front, where, on a large board and easel, the teacher had pinned a piece of thin paper, off-white in colour, called kitchen paper. Each child had a similar sheet, and also on each table were some paint pots and brushes. The teacher picked up her brush and told the children to watch her carefully, and not to touch their own brushes yet. She then painted a blue brush stroke in the right-hand top corner of her paper, turned to the class and told them to do as she had done, all to start in the top corner nearest the door. But one small boy had jumped the gun! He had picked up a brush, dipped it in red paint and drawn a bold stroke across the bottom of his paper. When the teacher noticed this she became very angry, telling the whole class how stupid he was. The class sat petrified, and so did we four adults. The miscreant shrank in his seat. Later when the class had been allowed to complete their paintings, we visitors went around and admired the finished work. I noticed that my companions, like me, made a point of being particularly complimentary to the offender. We were all so sympathetic that he insisted we took his picture with us. We visited other classes that afternoon, and while none was so forbidding as the first, none was inviting either.

We said our farewells politely and left. Once a decent distance away from the school, we stopped in the street and breathed sighs of relief. We all had the same thought: if we had to attend that school we would also be wetting our pants – and we were teachers! We could have told the headmistress that we had solved the mystery of her enuretic children, but we lacked the courage. It is a comfort to think that the teachers we saw that day will have long been retired from teaching.

This was the worst example of teaching as telling that I ever came across. Not all schools which have a didactic approach are so insensitive and thoughtless as that one was, but I often wonder about the aims of such teachers and I am amazed at their immense self-confidence in believing themselves always to be right and demanding that only *their* ideas be followed. I have also come across parents who are forever *telling* their children what to do and when to do it. So often these parents complain later when their children are young adults that their offspring lack initiative and can't do things for themselves.

Buttercups and ponies

Some, even most, primary teachers nowadays organise their classes into groups, which are given a variety of names, from simple colours to the more poetic flowers or animals. Such classes look less formal, but sometimes these are ability groups, arranged so that those children thought by the teacher to be the most able are gathered together to do more advanced work, those thought the least able are given less challenging work, and intermediate groups are given intermediate work. It is rather like having a number of small streamed classes in one classroom. This form of organisation completely overlooks all the research on teachers' self-fulfilling expectations and the effect of streaming on pupils' motivation.

I have too often seen classrooms in which children are sitting in groups, around three or four tables put together to make a working area, but are still expected to copy work from a blackboard. Those sitting at right angles have to turn their heads 90 degrees, but those sitting with their backs to the board actually have to squirm round 180 degrees, then turn back to write, twist round again for a further sighting, and so on, until the difficult task is done, and usually without any complaint – just another strange thing one is asked to do in school! So things are not always what they seem at first glance, and groups do not a progressive classroom make . . .

Probably most teachers use groups in order to manage classes which are too large, feeling that whole-class teaching is somewhat infra dig. By dividing the class into four or five groups, they can concentrate on the work of two or three groups each day. The work supervised by the teacher is likely to be language or mathematics. Other groups will have tasks set which are largely self-correcting, so that they are able to work with minimum supervision. The work of such classes has to be tightly organised so that children are not wasting their time; before school, teachers spend a great deal of time each day laying out the activities with which a maximum number of children will usefully be able to occupy themselves.

The type of activities will vary according to the age of the children. In a young infant class there might be a table for jigsaw puzzles and another for junk modelling while a third area will be arranged for painting; three or four children may be playing in a 'house corner', two or three with water, others with sand; floor activities will include constructional activities with bricks or Lego. Some children will be looking at books, and/or listening to a story on cassette while another group may be weighing or sorting things into sets, and others will be writing. There might well, nowadays, be a computer in a corner with two or three children working on a simple program. The teacher will be able to concentrate, for short periods, on the group writing, or the groups pursuing mathematical activities, and will be mentally checking on the activity of all the individual children.

In a class of older children the teacher will be able to plan for longer periods of concentration. Perhaps a teacher wants to develop the concept of place value with a particular group. Other groups might be working on work sheets with number puzzles, or dictionary searches, which should occupy most of them for 20 or 30 minutes. A few others are making closely-observed drawings of plants growing in the room. Another group might have been asked to estimate the weights of a group of objects, weigh them and then compare their estimates with the recorded weights, with a view to making a graph of their estimates aginst the actual weights. If the teacher is concerned that all the children are working gainfully and purposefully, all these activities will have been carefully prepared and the preparation will have taken some hours of the teacher's time either before or after school.

Such groups might be organised as ability groups, i.e. streamed, or as friendship groups, or flexible groups. If the last, the structure of the groups would vary, depending to some extent on children's choice of activity and partly on the teacher's view of what activity a particular pupil needs to pursue in his or her own interest. The groups might be collaborative, or the members of a group might be working independently of one another, although engaged on similar tasks, their combination as a group entirely due to the teacher's need to split the class into manageable units.

Whether or not this method of working is successful depends very much upon the teacher's efficiency as an organiser in planning out group and individual tasks, recording the work done by the groups and monitoring what the individuals in the groups have produced.

Shift workers

Some teachers who organise their classes into groups determine upon a period of time and have each group working in an area of the curriculum for this set period. At the end of the fixed time the children are told to put away what they have been working on and move to their next task. Sometimes this means a physical shift to another part of the classroom. The teacher might either circulate between groups or perhaps have one of the groups reading to him or her for each fixed period. The chief problem with working in this way is that not all the children are likely to complete their tasks in the set time. Those who finish early often get bored and/or disruptive, while those who have not finished to their own satisfaction become frustrated. It is an inflexible system and I have seen children become very alienated when working in this way.

Working together

There *are* classes, however, where groups are more than an organisational device: these are classes where collaborative learning is part of the teacher's aims. There, children are likely to be grouped according to the task before them: if they are given an opportunity to master a new process, their next task might be to share their new skill by demonstrating what they have learned to other groups, as individuals or in pairs. The composition of groups will be subordinated to the needs of the tasks – which will often be determined by the children in consultation with the teacher.

If we think of a group of ten-year-olds, perhaps working together to write a puppet play, there would be discussion first and probably argument. Perhaps the teacher will be asked to decide between the themes proposed by different members. Probably the teacher will, by asking questions about how the themes could be translated into action, encourage the children to decide for themselves which theme would be the most practicable and interesting. They would have to agree on the number of characters and write a script. Whoever was the fastest and clearest writer would no doubt be appointed scribe. Once the script was written, they would have to decide which of them would speak the different characters. Costumes and scenery would have to be made, and the play rehearsed. Finally there would be a performance for the rest of the class. There might be a demand for the play to be rewritten as a story, illustrated, and made into a book for others in the class and school to read. Once again, the members of the group would have to decide which part of the book they would work on, in collaboration.

Or it might be that two children choose to work together on a scientific enquiry, perhaps making electrical circuits, and finding out whether or not different ways of connecting them can affect the brightness of a torch bulb. When they have experimented and formed a theory, they will be able to explain this to others in their class. Then the others will want to test the theory for themselves. Together, they can learn more than by a competitive race to see who can do what first. When they are competing, it is the competition that becomes important, not the learning they are engaged in.

When children collaborate to solve problems they call upon a range of skills which they possess in combination, and children who are less competent at a task, can, by working with those more adept, learn from their colleagues and improve. Then they can, in their own turn, demonstrate their own skill in some other field, and, from pupil, become teacher. There will also be class sessions, when new findings are shared with the whole class. These findings may be turned into books or classroom displays; sometimes they will form the basis for an assembly project and shared with the whole school.

Children working in this way will be encouraged to articulate their thoughts, make hypotheses and test them against reality; there will be a more scientific approach engendered in such classrooms. Such students are likely to be more self-motivated and nonconformist. They will be used to situations where there is not always a right or wrong answer, and where the teacher will not always be right either. For teachers in such classrooms must also be able to say that they do not know everything, but that they, like the children, can find out. Children in such classes will certainly spend more time *thinking* than will children in a class taught by a didactic teacher.

In order to offer more challenge to children's thinking, teachers have been pressed to use more 'open-ended' questions with pupils, which depend on the child's judgement. Thus, if a child is asked to give his or her reasons for liking or not liking a book, there can be no right or wrong answer. So too, if a child is asked to map the best route between two places, it could be the shortest route that is mapped, or it could be that a route which avoids dangerous main roads is mapped in preference, or the one with the most pleasant view: which route is *best* depends on judgement and circumstances. Only by allowing children in school to make judgements and take decisions will they learn to improve these important skills.

Vertical and horizontal grouping

This kind of grouping is usually decided as a matter of school policy. Vertical grouping is the name given to the form of class organisation in which the children have ages which extend over a period of more than one school year. In some schools at the 5-7 stage, children in the three age groups are in one class: each year the oldest children move out and new younger children join the class, while the other two years each move up one level. In some schools only two age groups are combined and some schools extend this into the 7-11 age range and have lower and upper junior classes. There was a lot of evidence presented some years ago to demonstrate the advantages of this form of organisation. More recently it has been found that children in mixed-age classes achieve less highly at junior level. I suspect much depends upon particular schools and teachers. In my experience a two-year period with the same teacher, so long as there was a good relationship between teacher and pupil, was positive for pupils, especially the youngest children. At the older end of the school, it was advantageous to have vertical grouping because the younger group matured more quickly in a class with the 11-year-olds, while the older group became more responsible, simply through having a younger age group with them. So much of teaching depends on a good pupil-teacher relationship at this age that it is an advantage for the vast majority of children to be with a teacher with whom they feel secure during their last years at primary school.

Horizontal grouping is the organisational form in which all children born between two dates, usually 1st September and 31st August, are taught as one class. This may seem very sensible, but in practice it is not always ideal. Children may have to change teachers each year, or, if the teacher keeps the class for two years this could be too long – unlike in a vertically-grouped class where the composition of the class changes each year and the class is never the same either for teacher or children in both years. Another area of potential difficulty is that there can be a tendency to assume that children in the same year group will have roughly equivalent levels of ability; this is not so. There can be tremendous differences – recent research indicates that in mathematics there can be as much as a seven-year gap between the most and least able.

Team teaching

This involves a combination of classes, either parallel, i.e. of the same age, or of different ages, and co-operation between teachers. If two classes, each of 27 children (the class size on which ILEA staffing is based), are to be taught in this way, there might be two or preferably three teachers involved. Sometimes a part-time teacher is included. Teachers who can offer particular skills can reach a larger number of children than when they work with only one class. Children can be divided into groups of 18, or 13 and 14, depending on the number of teachers available. In this way they can have more individual attention, but the whole class can, in turn, cover the same curriculum. This way of working involves a lot of forward planning: in most cases I have known, the teachers meet early each morning to discuss the day's programme and arrange the rooms. They also need to meet and compare notes at the end of each day. As well as this, joint sessions are necessary for long-term planning. Of course other teachers do this as well, but it becomes more complicated when so many more people are involved.

Partial forms of such organisation involve co-operative teaching in which classes and teachers combine for certain activities. One example might be teachers combining two classes to see a film, with one teacher supervising, while the other teacher prepared for the follow-up activities, and then those activities being divided. One teacher with a particular talent for, perhaps, model-making works with one group of children while other children make a book under the guidance of the other teacher and, should a third teacher be time-tabled, a further group of children could develop another activity arising from the film they had seen, e.g. composing incidental music – if that teacher had that kind of expertise. Or teachers with vertically-grouped classes might group all the older children to hear a more advanced story, once a week, while the younger ones had a story with another teacher. If teachers are working together then a great deal of flexibility is possible and what happens will depend on the specialisms of the teachers involved.

In most primary schools there are some teachers with posts of responsibility for certain areas of the curriculum. If a teacher has a post for music, for example, but also teaches a class, he or she might work with other classes for set periods. If there is no teacher without a class, there would have to be an exchange of classes for that time, and the teacher coming in to take the music teacher's class would offer those children his or her own specialism or continue with work in basic subjects already begun. But this is less satisfactory than having the class teacher working with a specialist teacher so that the subject is integrated into the class work. This however depends upon adequate staffing in the school, as do so many improvements in education.

Learning from the ORACLE

A most important and influential research project has recently been conducted from the University of Leicester. Titled *Observational Research and Classroom Learning Evaluation* it has involved a number of educationalists, led by Professors Brian Simon and Maurice Galton, in research into primary classrooms within the junior age group, including an assessment of the effectiveness of different teaching styles.

Moving away from the unproductive dichotomy of progressive and traditional, they have divided teachers into six main groups according to their styles, and children into four groups according to the way they prefer to work. Children were observed for a period of one or two years before transfer to middle or secondary schools, and for a year after transfer, and were tested for progress, not only in basic skills but also in study skills, at the beginning and end of each school year.

Some teaching styles were found to be more productive than others, but no style was found to be the best for all areas of the curriculum. For example, although the style which relied almost entirely on individual work was generally one of the least effective, it proved to be the most effective when reading and comprehension progress was measured. Teachers who spent the most time interacting with the children were most successful at encouraging children's cognitive development in other curriculum areas tested.

Teachers refer to *cognition* and *cognitive development*. Cognition is knowledge or knowing in the widest sense, including sensation, perception, etc., and cognitive development relates to the development of the rational mind or intellect. For the greatest cognitive development all the child's abilities need to be engaged. Whereas the didactic teacher will make statements and tell, the child is required to be a passive listener and to make correct responses to questions, which frequently means quoting back the information relayed by the teacher. On the other hand, the teacher who is asking probing questions is encouraging children to *think* and put forward their own ideas or *hypothesise* and consider and discuss these ideas. The researchers found that the pupils who made the most progress had teachers who spent more time stimulating thought in their pupils, and while teachers differed in the ways in which they applied this stimulus, their efforts resulted in more thought-provoking, or higher order, discussions with their classes.

Lower-order interactions are those concerned with how and where children should set out written work, the width of margins, the provision of equipment, behaviour correction and so on. In a section headed *Effective teaching in the primary classroom* the following description is given:

> To relieve the monotony of number work [with older junior children], the teacher designed a numerical crossword puzzle where the clues consisted of multiplication and division sums. The children, however,spent most of the period drawing the crossword grid and shading in the appropriate squares . . . the teacher's interaction with pupils consisted mainly of low level class supervision statements telling children what to do, or paraphrasing the instructions already given . . . a distinguishing feature of the unsuccessful teachers was their relatively high use of this category. The observer also noted that while pupils were drawing the numerical crossword there were few reasons for questioning or giving feedback, because the intellectual demands of the task were minimal. (*Progress and Performance in the Primary Classroom*)

The authors go on to relate another occasion when the usual teacher was absent and had left work written on the board which another teacher who was covering the lesson was to supervise. The class was reluctant to begin and the substitute teacher had to walk round, trying to make them to get on with their work. Upon asking one of the pupils a question about the work he was supposed to be doing, which was on wave motion, he discovered that the pupil did not understand the work. The teacher then left the room and returned with a number of slinky coil springs, moved the children into groups which he encouraged to experiment with the springs and note the different wave patterns. He asked them to suggest ways of altering the wave patterns, suggest hypotheses and test them with the coils:

> Gradually a transformation overtook the classroom. What had earlier been an uninterested and bored class of pupils suddenly became actively involved and enthusiastic, as the teacher's own enthusiasm for the subject transferred itself to them. By the end of the period, the pupils had completed the work successfully tackling it with a sense of purpose, if not with quite the same enthusiasm with which they carried out the experiments.

When I read examples such as these, I am reminded of the time I spent learning to drive and wonder how I would have got on if, instead of being seated at the steering wheel from the first lesson, getting the feel of the car and observing at first hand the effects of my actions, I had had to read the textbook and answer questions based on memory alone. (In fact I did read the textbook, but only after I had gained some first-hand experience of driving a car.) Pestalozzi wrote in 1827: 'The first rule is to teach always by *things* rather than *words*.' (*Letters on Early Education*) This was the basis of the Pestalozzi 'object lessons' in which children were encouraged to discover the attributes of an object for themselves before being told where it came from, how grown or made, and how it was used; in other words, to develop their sensory perceptions as the first step towards full cognition.

This brings to mind an incident which occurred some years ago, when my daughters were at school. A friend of theirs had recently transferred to a well-known grammar school and we had been invited to her house for tea during the school holiday. The three girls were standing by a window feeding peanuts to the squirrels which were coming right up to the sill to take the nuts. One of them remarked that peanuts were also called monkey nuts because monkeys liked to eat them. My younger daughter turned to me and asked whether they had more names, and I told them that they could be called groundnuts, because of the way they grew. At this there was an exclamation of surprise from their young friend. 'Is that what groundnuts are? We've been learning about them in geography but I didn't know they were peanuts.' Here was a class of 11-year-olds, learning about groundnuts, one of the easiest things to provide for first-hand experience, yet not being given the opportunity to make this connection which would certainly have increased their involvement in the lesson being taught.

In the same way, John Dewey in *The School and Society* told of a visit to the town of Moline on the Mississippi river, where the local children, far from exploring their immediate environment, had difficulty in believing that the great and important river they had learned about in their textbooks was connected with the stream that flowed past their homes.

Friedrich Herbart, whose theory of learning has much in common with modern theories, stated that 'abstraction should take place from examples, from the observed, from the given, and through individual acts of induction'. He also wrote in his book *The Science of Education*:

> For that instruction which analytically or synthetically aims at clearness of elementary presentations, and therefore commences the essential work of education, we should seek in the most direct way to gain the child's activity. Mental activity is healthy too! Healthy as that of the limbs and internal organs; everything will be set in motion together.

So we see once again that these 'modern ideas' are really rather ancient. The famed Socratic method, chronicled by Plato, was based on the setting of problems for discussion, and the asking of probing questions for the students to answer, each answer giving rise to another question, forcing the students to think deeply and put forward their own hypotheses, for Socrates believed that only in this way, and not by receiving 'wisdom' would they learn to think clearly and make the knowledge their own. Which is rather what the ORACLE research also concludes.

6 | Does it make sense?

> There are some important aspects of learning to read which the child must teach himself because we do not understand them. (*Understanding Reading*, Frank Smith)

There is a growing belief among teachers that some of the techniques we have evolved in order to help children to learn to read may themselves be stumbling blocks for many of them. I use the phrase 'help children to learn to read' rather than 'teach children to read' because, like Frank Smith, I am not at all sure that reading *can* be taught. The role of the teacher is an enabling one – to facilitate the efforts of the learner. Teachers have sought ways of simplifying a very complex process, breaking it down into steps and teaching children to climb those steps, one by one. Yet the even more complex task of learning to speak has been accomplished by the child without the aid of such artifice.

Young children learn to speak by hearing others and imitating the sounds they hear. They constantly experiment with these sounds and with language constructions; the more speech they hear, the more they participate in conversation, the more examples they gather in order to make those generalisations which assist their language development. In this way they gain a knowledge of the purpose and structure of spoken language. When young children attempt a new formulation, we expect them to make mistakes, and I have already referred to the negative effect of adult ridicule at this stage. Nor is it necessary for the adult to repeat a childish formulation; the normal adult speech will in itself provide the model for the child. There has been a great deal of research which illustrates this process and anyone in contact with small children can observe it for themselves.

One thing which is quite obvious when children are learning to speak is their search for meaning. The acquisition of language gives the child more control over the environment, and most children have a natural urge to increase their independence and ability to act autonomously. But the words used have to have a meaning which is understood by the listeners. If the child wants a particular toy which it has named 'Boo', and parents and brothers and sisters understand this, the toy will be given to the child when that sound is made. But if the child is with someone who does not know that name, frustration will result. The stranger might finally, by trial and error, hit on the wanted toy and then say, 'Oh, you mean the train'. Eventually the child will add the word 'train' to his or her vocabulary because the meaning of this word is more widely understood – the word is more useful. Meaning is not something intrinsic, but is socially determined, and words are a kind of currency, the value of which is generally agreed and accepted.

Children also acquire an understanding of rules in our language which we take very much for granted, which no-one formulates for them, because we ourselves are so unaware of them. In his later book, *Reading*, Frank Smith gives the example of *small, blue, wooden sailing boat*, not *wooden, blue, small sailing boat* and points out that although we do not put this convention into words, few children over the age of five would get it wrong.

In his book *How Children Learn*, John Holt suggests that if we taught children to speak in the way we try to teach them to read, they might never learn. We would have analysed sounds, made lists of the commonest and would teach those first; we would have made lists of syllables and words:

> When the child had learned to make all the sounds on the sound list, we would begin to teach him to combine the sounds into syllables. When he could say all the sounds on the syllable list we would begin to teach him the words on our word list. At the same time, we would teach him the rules of grammar, by means of which he could combine these newly-learned words into sentences. Everything would be planned with nothing left to chance; there would be plenty of drill, review and tests, to make sure that he had not forgotten anything.

In this context this sounds ridiculous, yet it is precisely what is often done when children are learning to read. Some children have always managed to learn to read, it would seem, by themselves. What we probably mean when we say this is that, having had a wide early experience of books, having had many interesting and enjoyable stories read to them, having been encouraged to make sense of printed signs and captions in their environment, as on food labels and street signs, some children have had a rich enough early experience of the printed word to enable them to begin reading print with a minimum of further help from adults.

This is necessary for all our children, but those who come into school without this background of experience of the printed word and the pleasure to be gained from reading, might easily become confused about the purpose of these exercises when they are assailed by single words to be memorised, or given the task of learning individual letter sounds before books can be awarded. Stories will be read to them, but the message gets confused, especially when the story is frequently interrupted for the teacher to check the spelling and phonic make-up of words in the story, as I have seen one or two teachers doing. The contradictory messages being relayed to the child are a) stories are to enjoy and have a meaning; and b) the meaning is secondary to knowing how the words are spelt and knowing what sounds make up those words.

Helping the reader who encounters problems

Some children make very rapid progress when learning to read, others learn more slowly, but do progress, while a third group experiences serious difficulty. Whatever the reasons for the problems, the teacher needs to diagnose them, with the parents, and help the child to overcome them. Physical causes should always be checked – sight and hearing especially. The first step is to *listen* to the child's reading efforts and observe the errors being made without necessarily correcting them, because it is from the errors that we can gauge the strategies the child is using, and the mis-understanding from which the mis-reading is arising. If we merely correct the child, who copies the correction without understanding the reason for it, he or she will have no way of applying the lesson in other situations. There are various reading tests which can be used to analyse the difficulties. Sometimes if this level of analysis does not provide an answer, the help of an educational psychologist might be needed.

I remember having a seven-year-old boy sent to me by his teacher with a request for help with his reading. I knew him for a very bright child who had appeared to be reading quite fluently at five and six years of age. He had been very quick to grasp mathematical concepts during his early years. I asked him to read his reading book to me, noting that it was somewhat simple for a boy of his age and interest level. At one point in the reading I noticed he read 'blue' for 'green' and looked at him (I had been following the text in the book). To my surprise he was not looking at the book, but up at the ceiling! I asked him to stop reading and suggested that he had memorised the book. With a sigh of relief, he agreed. He had, he admitted, been deceiving us all for two years by learning his books off by heart; this was easier for him than actually decoding the print. While it had not been too difficult a task when he was being given simple early readers, as the books became more advanced, he was beginning to find it more and more difficult to carry through the deception, and had become very anxious about the outcome. I discussed the problem with his parents and suggested that as there was an educational psychologist in the school, I ask her to test him, and this was agreed.

The results of the test were very interesting, because while his auditory memory and perception were four years ahead of his age, his visual perception and memory were way behind. As a result of this information we were able to explain to the boy that he would always rely on his ears a great deal, but that if we worked out ways of helping him use his eyes to better effect, he would find reading easier. The most notable thing about the whole episode was the obvious lightening of his load; his face lit up when he found that we understood his difficulty and did not consider it insuperable, and that we were not angry with him for his deception. By concentrating on his strengths, and attempting to strengthen his weaknesses, he was helped, and became a good reader.

This boy received remedial help, in this case, from me, his headmistress. Other children who need extra help to remedy weakness in their reading development may receive this in various ways. Ideally small classes would enable class teachers to carry this work out within the classroom, but we rarely have such ideal situations. The ORACLE findings were that children made more progress with their reading when they were taught individually. In practice, many schools have teachers with a responsibility for giving assistance where children need such extra help. These teachers sometimes work in the classroom alongside the class teacher, or they might take small groups of children to work in a separate room. Where two teachers are working in this way, very close contact and monitoring of the children's progress is necessary so that there is no disruption of the continuity of their work.

It is obvious to teachers that large classes disadvantage those children who do face difficulties, who have special needs. These needs require diagnosis, and remedying, as did the reading problem of the boy quoted above. By and large such diagnosis, and sometimes the remediation too, needs a one-to-one situation, which is expensive. The children who can cope, those with books in the home, with parents who have time to devote to their child's development, will usually come from stable homes, where the interests of the children will be important within the family. Children coming from unstable homes, or from homes where books are rarities, or where even school library books are allowed to be torn up by the baby, or where video nasties may be permitted viewing, are going to be disadvantaged.

Children live in society; their lives are shaped by what is happening around them. If they are members of ethnic minorities and face racism, if they are poor and wear clothing which spotlights their poverty, if they live in sub-standard housing or are homeless, if they suffer from ill health and poor diet, their ability to learn to read may well be seriously affected. If they come from homes where anxiety about unemployment is paramount, and the concerns about jobs, income, homes, or the lack of them, are more real to the child than those of school, if they are worried about sickness or disruption in the family, they have special needs. All these children can only learn if enough adult time is invested in them. Schools exist in the social setting and it has been recognised in some local education authorities – the ILEA, for example – that the conditions in the inner cities are such that children growing up in them need additional resources to overcome those disadvantages.

Panaceas

Because of teachers' awareness of shortage of time, and the difficulty of the task they face in assisting the learning of large numbers of young children, sometimes without adequate equipment and books, they easily fall victim to commercial blandishments; the new scheme which will really get the children all reading seems very attractive. Many of these schemes can be seen in schools, having been bought some time in the past, but never really having paid for their keep in terms of usefulness to the children. Yet all these schemes are the result of expensive educational research; new methods are developed and publishing firms invest in these new schemes, which are advertised and sold to parents and teachers with the assurance that they will provide a new panacea. One of the more extreme examples of this was the Pitman Initial Teaching Alphabet scheme, which used a completely new alphabet for beginner readers. Having learned this alphabet, which they used both for reading and writing, they were then transferred to the orthodox alphabet. The reasoning was that our traditional orthography confused children. But all the incentives to reading – the cornflakes packets and the instructions for model making – were still printed in the old way, and there was no lasting evidence to show that the ITA did help children learn to read faster; its very artificiality seemed to many of us in teaching to be much more of a disadvantage. I do not know personally of one school where it is still being used, although there may well be several.

The mystique of the emperor's clothes

At the Eleventh World Congress on Reading, held in London in July 1986, John Merritt, former Professor of Educational Studies at the Open University, pointed out that teachers could not give children the attention and opportunities available in good homes – classes were too large. As a result, teachers took refuge in theory to make up for the lack of real experience they could provide: there was material available to explain every technique or method used in the teaching of reading.

As *The Times Educational Supplement* reported (1 August 1986), Professor Merritt said that there was little research to show that the panoply of expense was justified and none to show that one method of teaching was better than another. He wondered who was the expert when children were being taught to read before going to school, by those with no professional training. The time had surely come to ask whether the academic establishment was wearing the emperor's clothes.

The question asked by Professor Merritt is rather a good one, because so much of teaching is surrounded by a mystique, albeit one believed in sincerely by teachers and accepted by most parents. It is based on the fact of teacher training courses, the aura of mystery surrounding any intellectual activity, and adults' memories of the difficulties which they experienced as school children.

I remember an incident from my early years in infant teaching when I had a class of five- and six-year-olds, with many children who were able to overcome the confusion no doubt engendered by my asking them to 'bark at print' (as the automatic response to the stimulus of a word was termed) and apply phonics, according to the practice at that time, and who began to read fluently during their first year at school. They were all children who had had the advantages outlined above and had come into school 'ready to read'. At the first parents' evening, the mother of one intelligent little girl came to talk about her daughter's progress. She was full of admiration, she said, for I had managed to teach Marion to read very quickly. Yet each time she asked Marion what she had done at school that day, the child replied 'We played' or 'I painted.' I, no doubt blushing, replied truthfully that I could not have stopped Marion learning to read, had I tried, which I certainly had no wish to do. Her mother seemed quite put out by this response. At the end of the evening I was waylaid by my headteacher who asked me what I had said to Marion's mother, who had been to see her to tell her that if her teachers did not teach the children, there seemed no point in their coming to school! I explained, but was advised not to say things of that kind to parents; in other words, not to shatter the mystique!

The question, nevertheless, remains – how can we ensure that all the children coming into our schools gain the experience they need in order to read fluently and with pleasure? Marie M. Clay in her book, *Reading – The Patterning of Complex Behaviour*, published in 1979, wrote:

> In the last 15 years there has been an intensive search for better theories about the reading process. Theories should predict what will happen if we change our way of teaching. But our present theories compete for support rather than lead us to clear explanations and predictions. On the one hand the traditional, older view sees reading as an exact process with an emphasis on letters and words, while on the other hand a more recent set of theories sees reading as an inexact process, a search for meaning during which we sample only enough visual information to be satisfied that we have received the message of the text.

My only point of disagreement with Marie Clay is that I do not consider the view which sees reading as an 'inexact process' to be very recent. Since Comenius was writing that 'children should learn to write by writing and to reason by reasoning' in the 17th century, learning to read by reading is clearly in this developmental tradition. In fact he wrote that:

> In language teaching examples must precede rules since natural development consists of acting first and only afterwards reflecting on the circumstances of the action.

Through the eyes but *in* the brain

Both Frank Smith and Marie Clay emphasise in their work that we use as few visual clues as possible when reading because, as Frank Smith writes, the more non-visual material you have when you read, the less visual information you need, and vice versa. An easy book can be read faster, it can even be read in smaller print, and can be read in relatively poor light – just as the better you know someone, the easier it is to recognise that person from a distance. As children become more experienced readers, they become able to read books with smaller print and longer words, and no longer need to read every word, and are able to guess or predict more and more what will come next.

Thus visual and non-visual material can, to some extent, be substituted for each other, and this is critical because there is a severe limit to how much visual material the brain can handle. If the brain is thought of in terms of a computer, children learning to read are programming their own computers – building in patterns which can have different applications – in reading different books. Here too, errors have to be eradicated, and time must be allowed when children are reading aloud, for self-correction. Too often we, as adults, rush in to correct a mistake when all that is needed is to allow time for the child's brain to register the error and go back and correct it. Then the brain will have less difficulty reprogramming and eradicating the error than if we had done the correcting.

Prediction is an important part of reading, and the more experience we have of reading the more we are able do it successfully. This is why we so often miss errors when we read: we do not read each word; our concern is to extract the maximum of meaning with the minimum of visual contact. A simple experiment is to cover the lower half of one of these lines with a piece of paper. You will probably be able to read the line without any problem, simply by using the visual clues provided by the top half of the words. As Frank Smith makes clear, the eyes merely look; it is the brain which gives meaning to what the eye has looked at. And the brain interprets the visual contact in terms of its existing conceptual structures. So, driving along a road on a hot day and seeing what appears to be a pool of water ahead, an adult will be able to interpret that as a mirage, but to a young child without that concept it will seem to be a pool of water, and its non-materialisation as such will seem magical.

The brain can memorise meaningful statements which fit into an already existing conceptual structure, much more readily than it can memorise unrelated items. A sentence like 'The little dog laughed to see such sport' is easier to remember than eight un-related words – e.g. 'to, from, here, go, say, with, under, time' – or even the same words, arranged in an order which deprives them of meaning: 'see, laughed, to, sport, such, dog, little, the'. Incidentally, we may well wonder why nursery rhymes retain so much appeal for children. They do not have a controlled vocabulary and are, in fact, quite difficult to understand. Perhaps the circumstances in which they are heard at home, the fun and laugh-ter associated with them, make them popular with young child-ren? It is not unreasonable to assume, therefore, that young children's reading books should be books which they enjoy read-ing, which have meaning for them and which it is worth their while to read. This means that the same book will not be as valuable to every child, because different books will have different appeal for different children, although humorous books do seem to have almost universal approbation from young children.

The Times Educational Supplement of 1 August 1986 reported a project in Leicester on reading in which the use of 'real' books rather than reading schemes was shown to help slower learners to develop a more positive attitude towards reading. Forty-eight children from four inner-city primary schools took part in the project run by Margaret Litchfield, of the Leicestershire Literary Support Service.

Older children volunteered to help the younger ones, who were all poor readers, for 15 minutes daily, four days a week, from the previous September to December. All of the younger children had been on reading schemes. After three months, standardised test results showed that both the 'tutors' and their 'pupils' had made greater average gains in reading than did the children in the control group who had remained on reading schemes. Eighty-four per cent preferred the books they had been reading to their normal class reading books. All but one thought of themselves as better readers.

Another method is shown in practice in Sylvia Ashton Warner's book *Spinster*, in which she describes how as a teacher in a New Zealand school, she supplied the children with a tin each in which they kept a collection of words on pieces of card, words which they had requested while doing their daily writing. The following day she would listen to them read through these words and any they had not remembered from the day before were thrown away, because she felt these had no real meaning for the child. Next time one of these discarded words was asked for, it might be remembered, and then would form part of the child's vocabulary store. The meaningful words were the ones the child recognised, and went on recognising; these had emotional significance. It might seem that this method would limit the children's vocabulary, but this was not so, for learning to read is a *process* that goes on from day to day, week to week and year to year. Additional information is absorbed during the process, as and when it becomes appropriate. As an adult reader I am constantly acquiring new information about syntax, and new vocabulary, in the course of my reading. Had I tried to memorise this at an earlier date, before it had significance, the task would have been onerous and probably counter-productive.

Bi-lingual children

Many of the children Sylvia Ashton Warner was teaching were of Maori extraction, and for them English was a second language. In our own schools we have many children for whom English is a second language and there have been concerns expressed that the teaching of bi-lingual children might in some way adversely affect the teaching of other children. Some of these concerns arise from a lack of understanding of how children do learn, and learn from one another; some might have racist origins. Thousands upon thousands of children have grown up speaking two languages – this has been commonplace in Welsh schools, and I hope it will continue to be so. It would have been advantageous if in the past more of us had learned to speak other languages from an early age. It is important for all children to be well grounded in their own first language, because there is evidence that we all of us use our first language when we are absorbing a new concept, or wrestling with a new idea. Young bi-lingual children might take a little longer to become fluent, but when they do so, they are fluent in two languages – a decided advantage.

Developmental writing

Working on the lines of using more natural language with children, and concentrating on the process rather than the product, some teachers are encouraging children to write freely without worrying about spelling accuracy, while at the same time presenting the children with many correct models for them to read. This is done by having plenty of attractive published books available and by having teacher-made books of shared writing, that is, the group of children combine to make up the text, while the teacher prints out the captions. These big books are then used as further reading material.

The children are encouraged to predict for themselves how the words they want to use in their own writing will be spelled, using alphabet sounds – the sound values the letters have in the alphabet – and are not automatically given the correct spellings. While their early writings present decoding problems for adults, they make astonishing progress towards accepted spelling conventions, and, uninhibited in their writing, are able to concentrate on the content – the meaning of their writing – which they want to communicate to readers. Children working in this way begin to write their own books from the start. When they read their books, they give meaning to the arrangements of letters they have written. Gradually more and more recognisable words appear and the writing becomes easier for others to decode, but these books always have meaning for the authors.

The converse of this was noted by the Assessment of Performance Unit in their publication *Language Testing 1979-83*, which found that, by emphasising neatness and correct spelling, teachers gave pupils the impression that these were the most important aspects of their writing. Only one quarter of 11-year-old pupils in the survey thought that 'imaginations and ideas were important'. The report states:

> If they have been encouraged to feel that they are good, or reasonably good, writers, they will be pupils able to approach

new writing tasks with confidence.

One teacher, using developmental writing, told me that while it meant less writing down words in children's dictionaries, it was very demanding because 'You are more like a mum – it can't ever all get done'. The great advantage, however, was that the teacher was constantly interacting with the pupils and discussing their work with them, without the distraction of providing spellings for other children in the class. I once again refer back to the ORACLE research which pointed out the importance of teacher interactions for maximum pupil progress.

Getting it right – at the right time

At some stage, older children are going to want to present their work to others, whether other classmates, or their parents, or for public display. Then there is a real point in making corrections. Class and school magazines, made books and work for exhibition all provide incentives for editing and for checking spelling. In this way it makes sense to the children, because they can see the purpose. And if they have been encouraged to read and write with confidence they will be without that defensiveness which prevents us and them from seeing a mistake as something to learn from, something to be changed without an over-emotional response. But this is a stage which has to be reached; the youngest readers and writers have not built up the confidence needed and are liable to be seriously inhibited by constant correction.

Nurturing good readers

How can we ensure that our young become good readers? By surrounding them with attractive books from their earliest days; by reading to them, lovingly; by conversing with them and involving them in our activities as well as showing a willingness, by playing with them, to be involved in theirs; by answering their questions and listening to what they say, and by understanding that they are faced with a serious task – that of making sense of the world about them. Children's play is the means by which they attempt to create order out of their impressions of the outside world and is very much a learning situation. Play is a serious matter – which is not to say that it should be without laughter and fun – and through play children gain the confidence they need for tackling new challenges, such as reading print. If they have plenty of experience of print at home, and if they are confident about themselves and not afraid to try something new, for most of them reading should not present any serious problem. Something to avoid, however, is the prestige race: 'My child is on Book Four. Mrs Smith's child is only on Book Two.' For this reason alone, linear reading schemes in which children have to climb up all the rungs of the ladder one by one, would contribute more by their absence than by their presence. The child on Book Four, in these circumstances and with this kind of pressure, might well stay there and never become a fluent reader. Anxiety to maintain position could well prevent the taking of chances and the readiness to make the mistakes which have to be made in the process of learning. The child on Book Two might become convinced of his or her own worthlessness by overhearing such statements, and give up trying. What is important for all children is that they have plenty of opportunity to read the books which interest them, thus giving plenty of material for future development.

How do we select children's books?

Children need access to both fiction and information books; they need to browse, and to read with concentration. All books carry messages and some books have messages in terms of descriptions of violent actions, sexist and racist stereotypes, which we might not wish our children to receive. Some parents use a form of censorship but this is not possible for very long because children will be irresistibly drawn to what they feel is forbidden. There have been suggestions that certain books should not be available in school and public libraries, and since not every single book published is on the shelves, there must be an element of selection by every librarian and teacher.

Books are given virtue by society; they do not have this virtue automatically. If we want our children to live in a world in which we all treat one another with respect we will not present them with books that show black people as grotesque or inferior. In South Africa, or any other racist society, the view will be different and racist books will be given to children. Just because a book like *Little Black Sambo* has been available for years and has been enjoyed without critical thought by many readers, this does not make it sacrosant. A book is a conveyance for the writer's ideas, no more and no less. We all have to decide what ideas we recommend to our children, and our decisions may well change from one period to another. We do not offer our children pornographic books, so why should we offer them racist or sexist books?

There are nevertheless many books which for a variety of reasons we might feel we want to have available in the classroom or in the home (*Robinson Crusoe* is one I have heard discussed in this way) while still being aware that such books contain material of which we disapprove. If such books are not censored, but discussed with the young reader, making clear the reasons for our misgivings, and viewed in the light of the historical period in which they were written, then this can only assist the youngster to develop a critical faculty – an excellent outcome. Such issues need discussing with children, and if there are matters in books of which parents disapprove, their reasons can be explained. Books with positive messages about our multi-ethnic society and about respect for other people and books with black or female heroes can be found, and if children have access to these at the same time as being involved in discussion about their parents' beliefs and the situations in which they find themselves, they will have a good basis from which to develop their own judgement.

There are certain basic requirements for children's books: they should be clearly printed, in bold type, so that they are easy to read physically. They should be written in language which is readily comprehensible, but should contain words which the child has not met before, so that, in reading them in an easily understood context, the child can assimilate them. Children's books should not patronise their readers, nor write down to them, using babyish language and repetition.

Children who learn to read fluently and enjoy books will not only find study easier later on, but will have their whole future lives enriched by their access to literature.

7 | How long will it take a bath to empty when the taps are running?

I remember doing problems like this when I was at primary school, but I was truly surprised to hear a parent complaining that his child was not being taught to tackle such problems. The scene was a parents' meeting on mathematics, and all the classes had been working on different aspects of a maths theme, relating to traffic in the school area. The work produced had been displayed around the hall and included picture graphs by the five-year-olds, and all the stages of graphical representation up to a pie chart produced by 11-year-olds. There were examples of binary maths, decimals and percentages. Addition and subtraction, multiplication and division were shown in various ways, and several classes had applied problem-solving techniques to find solutions to real problems arising from the increase of traffic in the area. Children had measured roads and made models; they had tried out embryonic traffic control schemes and one-way systems; some had made working battery models of traffic lights. There had been work done on velocity and angles of incline. All in all it had been a challenging project.

The purpose of the meeting was to explain to parents the kind of mathematics the head and staff felt to be most valuable for our children. The Staff Inspector for Mathematics, Laurie Buxton, came to speak about the work and point out one or two interesting themes to the parents. Then came questions, and among them the comment noted above. In answer, the mathematics inspector asked: 'How often is a child likely to need to work that out? Have you ever needed to do so?' The father agreed that he had never been faced with that problem in a practical situation. On reflection I realised how very stupid it was to create a problem, to be worked out by manipulating symbols, about a situation which no one in their right mind would ever create. The problem was that if one filled a bath, pulled out the plug and left the taps running, how one could find how long it would take the bath to empty. My question was: what did it matter anyway? What possible *use* would the answer be? Could it be that one might need to know whether the bath might overflow and cause a flood? But if so, why not just turn off the taps? But perhaps they were stuck. In that case surely it would be more useful for children to learn how to turn off the water and how to locate the stopcock. All in all, a pretty useless problem for children to work on; so why was that father worried that his child was not going to have to solve it?

I think that to understand that parent's anxiety one needs to return to the mystique surrounding teaching and schools. This mystique applies even more to mathematics than it does to language teaching because large numbers of adults believe that they were not any good at maths at school, and have anxieties about their abilities in this field.

In a BBC *Horizon* programme dealing with this question, shown in May 1986, some scaffolding workers were asked if they had had to cover mathematics in their training. They replied negatively and said their training had been largely concerned with safety regulations, stresses and strains, and so on. They did not connect mathematics with the work they were doing, and when the interviewer pointed out a layout of pipes on the ground which made a right-angled triangle, and said that it looked like a bit of Pythagoras to her, they laughed, and said it was merely a 3-4-5. But a 3-4-5 triangle is, of course, an application of Pythagoras' theorem! In the same programme, students at a fashion college were shown measuring patterns and adapting them by the use of ratios. They too were asked if their work didn't involve a lot of mathematics – and denied it. One of the best home dressmakers I know, whose clothes always fit her perfectly, is at the same time someone who says that she is terrified of maths and can't even add up! So why is it that so many adults, using mathematics efficiently in their everyday lives, believe that those activities and calculations they carry out have nothing to do with mathematics?

I believe it arises from the way the subject has been taught in the past, from the difficulty children have had in understanding new concepts *without sufficient practical experience*. Then later, when they learn practical maths in their jobs, because the work they did in school was so irrelevant, they do not perceive any connection.

The significance of practical work

Practical work is essential throughout the primary years if the primary curriculum is to be developed ... it is, though, necessary to realise at the outset that such work requires a considerable amount of time. However, provided that the practical work is properly structured with a wide variety of experience and clear stages of progression, and this is followed up by the teacher by means of questions and discussion, this time is well spent. (*Mathematics Counts*. Report of the committee of inquiry into the teaching of mathematics in schools, under the chairmanship of Dr W.H. Cockcroft, 1982)

Mathematics is very widely seen as concerned with the manipulation of symbols, a purely academic and intellectual pursuit, something done in the mind. But as Comenius wrote: 'Nothing is found in the mind which has not first passed through the senses'. The basic requirements can only be developed by the child through first-hand experience. As Jean Piaget wrote in *The Growth of Logical Thinking*:

When we speak of experience, we must distinguish two different types, which will help us see that a child learns very little indeed when experiments are performed for him, and that he must do them himself rather than sit and watch them done. . . .

In the realm of education . . . this means that school children and students should be allowed a maximum of activity of their own, directed by means of materials which permit their activities to be cognitively useful. In the area of logico-mathematical structures children have real understanding only of what they invent themselves and each time we try to teach them something too quickly, we keep them from re-inventing it themselves. Thus there is no good reason to try to accelerate this development too much: the time which seems to be wasted in personal investigation is really gained in the construction of methods.

This is saying very much the same thing: let children have time to think for themselves – as was emphasised in the chapter on reading and writing. Give the children time to think for themselves, time to program their own computers. Acceptance of what they are told by an adult prevents children from developing their own mental structures.

Many parents visiting their child's first classroom feel disappointed if they do not find books filled with 'sums'. Yet such sums, while they are exercises in writing, often have nothing whatever to do with early mathematical learning. If they are the result of children copying from a card made by the teacher and writing down the result, correct answers do not mean that the child has gained understanding of the arithmetic. Only if the child has been working with apparatus of some kind – pencils, milk cartons, blocks, sticks, toys, counters – and arrived at the answers by manipulating things which are real to the learner, will the idea of the number have significance. This may read as if it is a new idea, but it is not. It had been advocated by Comenius, and Pestalozzi wrote in his *Letters on Early Education*:

> Experience has shown that those very children who had acquired the first elements in the concrete . . . had two great advantages over others. First they were perfectly aware, not only of what they were doing, but also of the reason why. They were acquainted with the principle on which the solution depended; they were not merely following a formula by rote; the state of the question changed, they were not puzzled, as those are who only see as far as their mechanical rule goes, and not farther.

Pestalozzi also noted that their understanding made these children more competent in mental calculations.

In Britain, a book was published in 1836, *Education Reform*, written by Sir Thomas Wyse, who was then MP for Tipperary, which advocated that children should use:

> Always something visible and tangible. Additions and subtractions should be performed always in reference to real objects.

When parents find children using a variety of methods in multiplication and division instead of following the rules by which they themselves were taught, (even though those rules might have become a bit hazy), they become anxious about 'modern methods'. Yet Sir Thomas Wyse wrote the following 150 years ago:

> For a considerable period . . . the pupil will continue to perform all his multiplications by repeated additions and his divisions

by repeated subtractions . . . he will gradually, of himself, abridge these methods, and fall at last into the invention of a multiplication table.

Learning is essentially learning to do something *for oneself* and children have to do things for themselves in order to improve their ability to do them well. And children's interest is often aroused by the solution of practical problems. It is interesting to note that Rousseau, who is commonly thought of as an advocate of absolute freedom, proposed a very structured mathematics and science programme in his book, *Emile*, written in 1762:

> Measure, count, weigh, compare. Do not use force till you have the resistance; let the estimation of the effect always precede the application of the means, get the child interested in avoiding insufficient or superfluous efforts. If in this way you train him to calculate the effects of all his movements, and to correct his mistakes by experience, is it not clear that the more he does the wiser he will become?
>
> Take the case of moving a heavy mass; if he takes too long a lever he will waste his strength; if it is too short, he will not have strength enough; experience will teach him to use the very stick he needs . . . Does he know how to compare masses of like substance and different size, or to choose between masses of the same size and different substances? He must set to work to compare their specific weights. I have seen a young man, very highly educated, who could not be convinced, till he had tried it, that a bucket full of blocks of oak weighed less than the same bucket full of water.
>
> It is only by walking, feeling, counting, measuring the dimensions of things that we learn to judge them rightly; but on the other hand, if we were always measuring our senses we would trust to the instrument and would never gain confidence. Nor must the child pass abruptly from measurement to judgement . . . I would . . . have his first estimates tested by measurement, so that he may correct his errors, and if there is a false impression left upon the senses he may correct it by a better judgement. The same natural standards of measurement are in use everywhere, the man's foot, the extent of his outstretched arms, his height. When the child wants to measure the height of a room,

his tutor may serve as a measuring rod; if he is estimating the height of a steeple let him measure it by the house; if he wants to know how many leagues of road there are, let him count the hours spent in walking along it. Above all, do not do this for him; let him do it himself.

Rousseau's excellent advice should be taken seriously by parents. In a child's early years there are many everyday situations which give the kind of experience which facilitates mathematical understanding. One example is table laying. If there are four chairs around a table a child could be asked to lay a place for each chair. He or she will probably take a handful of forks and put one at each place; then fetch knives and match one knife to one fork, and the same with spoons. After completing this task many times, the child might begin to predict how many of each item will be needed, and take four forks, four knives and four spoons. By handling these sets of four enough times, the child has begun to develop the concept of four as O O O O or 1111, and can retain that concept in mind so whenever he or she meets the word four, or sees the symbol 4, the meaning has consistency. This will happen more easily if other opportunities to bring the quantity to the child's notice have been taken. The characteristic of four-ness will have become clear to the child, and this process has to be repeated with all the numbers, until the child reaches the stage of being able to think in a more abstract mode.

Before their mathematical thinking can mature, children need to establish for themselves the concept of conservation. This was stated by Piaget to be 'the necessary condition for all rational activity' and it requires the child to be quite certain that if nothing is added to nor subtracted from a quantity, that quantity will remain the same, no matter how it is arranged. For example, two equal sets of blocks are placed on a table before the child, as illustrated in figure 1. The child can then match them one-to-one and is asked if they are the same, or if one has more blocks than the other. The child will count them and agree that they are the same. Then, in front of the child, they are rearranged as illustrated in figure 2:

| Fig. 1. | Row A | □ □ □ □ |
| | Row B | □ □ □ □ |

| Fig. 2. | Row A | □□□□ |
| | Row B | □   □   □   □ |

If when the child is asked again he or she states that Row B has more blocks, simply because there is more space between the blocks, then we can assume that the child has not yet stabilised the concept of conservation in spatial terms. If on the other hand the child is quite sure that four blocks remain four blocks, however they are moved around, we can feel confident that the child has understood the principle of conservation and can move on to other mathematical problems. The child who is not sure about conservation needs much more experience of handling and arranging different quantities in order to establish this concept.

Piaget devised numerous other conservation tests, including some on the conservation of volume, and these are now widely used in primary classrooms. The more purposeful experience children have and the more they are encouraged, through discussion, to reflect on that experience, the more readily will they be able to stabilise the principle of conservation.

I only played

It is common for young children, when asked to recount their day at school, to say 'I played'. But it is this 'play' which can enable the child to have just those experiences which will lead to mathematical development. Of course play is important for *all* curriculum areas, because it is during play that the child tests out hypotheses about language, behaviour, and his or her idea of the world. When children are playing with water, they are also learning about the behaviour of liquids and the capacities of different containers; when playing with bricks they are finding out about structures and shape; by their handling of different materials they learn about the behaviour of those materials in different conditions, about weight and density. They are learning cognitively, using their senses and all their perceptions, at a stage in their development when they can learn best from concrete first-hand experience.

This does not mean, though, that adult intervention is never warranted at this time. It is the adult who organises opportunities for constructive play: parents buy toys, make sandpits, make play space available; teachers organise the classroom activities, collect junk for modelling, cut paper for painting, check equipment for use with sand and water and in the house corner. The intervention of the teacher, raising questions for the children to pursue, directing the children's attention to paths from which they could draw their own conclusions, is most important and it requires sensitive observation of the children and an understanding of each child's level, of his or her strengths and weaknesses. This important task is made much more difficult when classes are large: it means that some children cannot receive this kind of adult intervention at a critical time. Important opportunities for assisting a child's mathematical development can be lost, simply because there is no-one available at a time when, if the child's attention were directed to a particular aspect, the principle of conservation could become apparent to him or her.

Some say that for children to discover for themselves there must be no adult help. In *Young Children's Thinking*, by Almay et al, this point is disputed:

> The child comes to an understanding of the world through his own efforts. While he may accommodate his thoughts to the ideas of others, it is only as he tries out those ideas within the context of the ideas he has previously acquired, that he makes them his own. *But there is no reason to believe that discovery is more meaningful if the child has to flounder aimlessly for a period before making the discovery.*

The emphasis is mine, because I think it is essential that adult intervention and help is available for the child. The ORACLE research showed the importance of teacher-child interaction and discussion for older junior children: it is perhaps even more vital for younger children, and that is why large classes in the early years of schooling are so injurious to children's development. But adults working with children should remember that telling children answers before they have had time to think problems through, is not helpful. Far from saving time, it leaves them unable to tackle those kinds of problem independently on another occasion; it might well leave them with a sense of inadequacy – 'I can't do it' – which might inhibit them in tackling problems in other areas as well. Confidence grows with success, and as adults we need to ensure that young learners are successful, otherwise we are merely sabotaging their efforts.

What kind of understanding?

Richard Skemp, formerly Professor of Educational Theory at

Warwick University, developed and expanded the notion, which was first introduced by Stieg Mellin-Olsen, of two kinds of understanding in mathematics: *relational*, in which one understands the relationships underlying mathematical formulae, and can apply those formulae in various situations, and *instrumental* understanding, which is all that is demanded in many schools, and comes from learning by rule. An example of this is the division of fractions: 7/8 ÷ 1/4 is solved by turning 1/4 upside down and multiplying, i.e. 7/8 x 4/1. If you understand why this is done, then your understanding is relational. But if you just know that that is the way to do it, and not *why*, then your understanding is instrumental. The notion of 'borrowing' in subtraction is another instance of this: why does it work?

In an article in *Mathematics Teaching* in December 1976, Skemp gives an example of instrumental understanding and the errors into which it can lead children. A class had learned the formula that area = length x breadth, and had worked a number of examples symbolically. When a student teacher was working in that classroom, she became suspicious about the pupils' understanding of area and asked them to find the area of a field 20 centimetres by 15 yards. No one queried these dimensions, and an answer of 300 square centimetres was given. The children were asked why the answer was not 300 square yards, and their reply was that 'Areas are always in square centimetres'! Skemp makes the point that if one is going to teach by rule, one must remember to teach all the relevant rules: in this case the rule that both dimensions must be in the same unit had been omitted.

The alternative, and the better option I believe, would have been for the children to have explored the question of area at some length, by covering surfaces in a variety of ways until they knew that an area was the space between boundaries, by using squared paper and counting the squares within a given boundary. Questions by the teacher could have helped to direct their attention to a relationship in rectanguar shapes, between the length and breadth of the boundary and the area calculated, and in that way the formula would be reached and understood as a useful short cut which could be applied in many situations. But when it is used, the practical basis would be understood, so that errors like the one above would not be so likely to occur.

Although instrumental understanding in children can give rise to neat pages of correct sums, pleasing to a parent's heart, it cannot lay the basis for mathematical development. While it may take longer to do the practical work necessary for relational understanding, once grasped this is not lost. It doesn't have to be remembered as a series of separate rules, but forms a mental network from which items can be retrieved as they are needed. Learning by rule, perhaps for an examination, relies on short-term memory and the knowledge is soon irretrievably lost to us – what a waste of time and effort. I know I got full marks in a trigonometry examination, because I had a good short-term memory – but I remember nothing of it now. Most adults I speak to admit the same, even those whose school-leaving examinations were more recent than my own. But do we really want our children to go on learning in this way?

One of the problems Richard Skemp raised in his article is the mismatch which occurs when a pupil who only wants to learn instrumentally is being taught relationally. Even more serious though is the situation where teaching is instrumental while a pupil needs to develop relational understanding, without the framework of which the rules being taught cannot be remembered. I suspect this is often the case and leads to students becoming turned off mathematics because they can no longer understand what they are being taught. Perhaps one of the chief causes of this is the number of teachers of mathematics who have themselves only instrumental understanding.

One method or many?

Several years ago, headteachers of primary schools in the area in which I was working were called to a meeting at a local boys' secondary school, one with a prestigious reputation in the locality and one to which we sent very many of our 11-year-old boys as did other local primary schools. There a proposal was put to us that, in order to simplify their mathematics work and make it easier for them to use the blackboard in their teaching, all the primary schools sending boys to them should agree on one method to be used for arithmetical operations. Thus all their intake would know the same rules and do their sums in the same way. The primary teachers were quick to point out that they thought this the antithesis of mathematics: that we felt it was essential that children learned that there were more ways than one of arriving at correct answers, and that we encouraged children to work out their own methods.

Our aim was to help children to think flexibly, not apply rules parrot fashion.

What we were arguing about was relational versus instrumental teaching. The secondary teachers, concerned with their examination results, wanted children to get right answers and good examination marks. In the primary schools we were already aiming at our children achieving relational understanding, although as teachers many of us were not too confident about our own understanding. And I believe we were correct, because if future generations are to develop the technological and scientific expertise that we are told is vital, then relational understanding of mathematics is going to be necessary.

There has been an increasing emphasis on problem-solving techniques in schools recently. This involves understanding of how and when to apply rules, and which rules will apply in particular situations. It also requires creative thinking and a willingness to explore a problem and make guesses or hypotheses – these are really the same sort of venture but the second sounds more impressive. It is a process which takes time and it is a process which is often more successful when attempted by a group, because group dynamics and feedback can stimulate the kind of thinking needed. It also removes pressure for a correct solution from the individual, thus making reasoning easier.

Quick as a flash . . .

In his book *Do You Panic About Maths*, Laurie Buxton, formerly ILEA Staff Inspector for Mathematics, demonstrates how negative emotions engendered by instrumental teaching get in the way of mathematical reasoning. He also points out that speed is not a necessary ingredient of mathematical thinking, and that many people get into a state of panic when presented with a problem in mathematics because they feel they have to produce an immediate answer which, if they cannot, or if they get it wrong, diminishes them as people. A number of case studies illustrate his thesis, and explain how his subjects overcame their disabilities. One I know was helped considerably and became a very successful teacher of mathematics; her earlier difficulties no doubt increased her sensitivity to the difficulties being encountered by her pupils.

He offers two views of mathematics. The first:

1. Fixed, immutable, external, intractable, and uncreative.
2. Abstract and unrelated to reality.
3. A mystique accessible to few.
4. A collection of rules and facts to be remembered.
5. An affront to common sense in some of the things it asserts.
6. A time-test.
7. An area in which judgements not only on one's intellect but on one's personal worth will be made.
8. Concerned largely with computation.

The second list postulates that mathematics is:

1. Experimental, exploratory and creative.
2. Abstract at times but often directly related to the most practical of problems.
3. Open to all but (as with all areas of study) to be penetrated more deeply by some than others.
4. A network of consistent relationships, easily remembered when understood.
5. Always reconcilable with the internal logic of the mind.
6. A contemplative subject requiring concentrated and undivided attention at times, but almost never needing to be done in haste.
7. An area in which judgements on one's ability should carry no more weight than in other studies.
8. About relationships in general.

The second list is a much more useful way of looking at mathematics.

The element of time pressure is one which is important in schools too. What used to go by the name of mental arithmetic, like oral table tests, required instantaneous answers. Because a child needs more time, it does not mean that he or she cannot work out the answer, yet slower children were always made to feel stupid. Laurie Buxton gives a much better picture of what mental maths should be about when he tells one of his subjects to 'spend time stabilising the problem', i.e. hold the visualisation of the problem in the mind and get it firm, view it from every angle until you can recall it at will. It is most important that there should be no pressure of time disturbing this process, because that anxiety about time gets in the way of one's reasoning ability. And in solving problems mentally we use many methods.

Those methods which we are taught as 'pencil and paper' methods, are not always the ones which we use when working mentally. Very often then, the rules we learned are discarded, and we calculate like the children quoted by Sir Thomas Wyse. This can be easily checked. How would you multiply 125 by 42 in your head? Would you multiply 125 by 2 units and then 4 tens? Or would you tackle it differently, say by multiplying 40 x 100 + 40 x 25 = 5000 and then adding the 250 got from 2 x 125? Or some other way altogether? Perhaps, if you were only given an instrumental understanding you would not be able to tackle it mentally at all, but would need pencil and paper! Test yourself to find out how you calculate under pressure of time, and how effective you are when that constraint is removed.

Using calculators

One quick way of checking a calculation is by the use of a calculator. There is a fear in some quarters that calculators will be seen by children as an excuse for not learning about numbers. This fear seems to be quite unfounded and is not based on what we know of children's curiosity. Calculators have become another way of working things out, and their use can stimulate children's interest in arithmetic. A child can be held back from learning about numbers because of fear of large numbers or the confusion caused by inaccuracies in computation. The use of the calculator can leave his or her mind free to learn about the processes involved and the relationships between numbers, which are important to understanding of the subject.

The child who is already interested in computation will be able to get great satisfaction from trying different combinations and operations which would be very time-consuming when done by hand. This is rather like doing one's washing in an automatic washing machine instead of hand-washing. A great deal of time is saved and far more washing can be done, but should the need arise, hand-washing can still be practised.

There is one very positive effect from the use of calculators: many young children find the concept of place-value difficult to grasp. They need a lot of practice with mathematical rods, for example, before they begin to understand. The calculator is a very valuable teaching aid for this concept: each time a number is multiplied by ten it moves to the left and the zero marks the place vacated. This helps the student to stabilise the idea of place-value.

Calculators should be widely available in schools, as recommended in the report of the Cockroft Committee. Their availability is limited by lack of finance.

Ways of thinking

Piaget formulated a theory of developmental stages in children's thinking:

The *sensory* motor phase – the first 18 months of life in which the infant moves to recognition of objects and sequences.

The stage of *symbolic* thought – from 18 months to four or five years: in which the child develops an inward model of the world through imaginative play, exploration, experiment, questioning, observation and imitation.The model is very unstable, and the child's thinking is very much in the 'here and now'.

The threshold of *operational* thinking – from about five to seven or eight years, a period when pre-conceptual thought changes and becomes articulated, when the concept of conservation is first approached.

The stage of *concrete* operations, from seven to 11 or 12 years, in which conservation becomes stabilised in a whole number of mathematical areas. Systems of reasoning begin to develop until the individual is able to operate without the concrete objects and experiences on which he or she has been dependent.

The stage of *formal* operations, from 12 to 15 years, when hypothetical reasoning can take place without the need for trial and error.

The problem which arises from Piaget's formulation is that the experiences of children, and the environment in which they live, can have a marked effect on their cognitive development. The ages which Piaget gives are based on his experience with a particular group of children. There are many, many pupils in this country who have not reached the level of formal operations by the age of 15, because they have not had the experiences and teaching which would help them to do so. It may be in some cases that their teachers expect them to have done so and teach them as if they had reached that level of reasoning. If adolescents and even some adults remain in the stage of concrete operations, this would help to explain some of the problems which arise.

Jerome Bruner, a prominent American psychologist, prefers to think in 'modes', and in his book *Toward a Theory of Instruction* he outlines three which will 'translate experience into a model of the world'. The first is through action: he calls this *enactive*:

> We know many things for which we have no imagery and no words, and they are very hard to teach anybody by the use of either words or diagrams and pictures. If you have tried to coach somebody at tennis or ski-ing or to teach a child to ride a bike, you will have been struck by the wordlessness and diagrammatic impotence of the teaching process.

The second depends upon sight and the other senses and upon the use of summarising images – and this Bruner terms *iconic*:

> We may . . . grope our way through a maze of toggle switches, and then at a certain point in overlearning, come to recognise a visualisable path or pattern.

Finally, there is representation in words or language – and this is abstract or *symbolic* in nature (not to be confused with Piaget's symbolic phase).

According to Bruner, the adult retains all three modes of thinking and different modes will be dominant at different times: when adults are tackling a new learning experience – learning to drive, for instance – they may need to pass through the enactive and iconic modes, before becoming expert in the new field. Although cognitive development moves through the earlier modes into the symbolic, Bruner suggests that learning which takes place only at the symbolic level may have drawbacks:

> When the learner has a well-developed symbolic system it may be possible to by-pass the first two stages. But one does so with the risk that the learner may not possess the imagery to fall back on when his symbolic transformations fail to achieve a goal in problem solving.

Using the idea of Bruner's modes of thought, it is quite easy to see how, if teachers are teaching symbolically while children are still operating largely in the earlier modes, mismatches arise which obstruct learning. Following Bruner's more flexible approach, teachers, when introducing new work, could involve pupils of any age in appropriate activities which would allow them to learn more easily.

He suggests that the iconic mode could provide a basis for particular activities. However, once the learner reaches the stage of thinking in the abstract, he or she nonetheless continues to rely upon the stock of imagery built up en route to abstract mastery. It is this stock of imagery that permits a convenient and non-rigorous means of exploring problems and relating them to those already mastered. So again there is a drawback for those taught in the symbolic mode, who may be less successful at solving problems for which they lack the imagery developed in more primitive modes of thought.

Bruner goes on to suggest that only an understanding of the earlier modes of thinking can help us to understand our own non-rational feelings and acts:

> There are various ways of processing information and the symbolic mode is one. Let me utter the suspicion that much of of the intrusive non-rationality about us, the disruptive forms as well as powerful ones such as the metaphors of poetry, derive from our iconic and enactive operations upon experience.

Who learns from a maths test?

Some tests, like the Piaget tests for conservation, are called diagnostic: they are valuable in helping a teacher decide at what level a particular child is reasoning, but they do not result in 'right' or 'wrong' answers. They are tests from which the *teacher* learns. Other tests, called attainment tests, test what the child knows, but marking answers right or wrong and adding up the marks does not tell anyone anything about the way a child is reasoning. A correct answer can be achieved in a particular example by quite faulty reasoning processes, which could result in incorrect assumptions being made by the child in the future.

The most dubious kind of test paper is the one which gives multiple choices, one of which has to be indicated by the examinee. A percentage of correct answers, perhaps not a high one – although this is by no means impossible – could be selected through pure chance. What anyone can learn from this process is questionable. As someone once said, no-one ever gained a pound by being weighed, nor grew an inch by being measured: neither can children learn by being tested.

Achieving mathematical literacy

Skemp's *instrumental understanding* and Bruner's *symbolic mode* both indicate the crucial need for first-hand experience and time to make knowledge one's own in the learning process. We return to problems at successive stages, as our mode of thinking changes, and look at them anew. Children need to handle and explore as many of the elements in their environment as possible. It will be on this basis of sensation and perception that their later understanding and skills will be based. Education, seen as a process, leads constantly to higher achievement. Seen only in terms of products, it polishes up the early products at the cost of restricting the whole process. We want too much too early, we want to see the products before our eyes, at a stage when the child is still struggling to establish basic concepts. I have seen five-year-olds sitting at tables and doing addition sums, writing symbols for quantities which they cannot even visualise. These children are learning to write the symbols, not learning mathematics, and neatness and rightness will for them usurp the place creative mathematical thinking should hold. It is rather like building a very smart house, without first making sure of good foundations, or decorating a room without preparing the walls first.

I hope it is clear from what has gone before that the question is not modern versus traditional maths. It is even possible, if a teacher does not understand what he or she is supposed to be doing, to work from a textbook which proclaims itself to be 'modern', and yet teach instrumentally, by telling children what to do, giving them the rules and the shortcuts, and not allowing them to try things out for themselves in a concrete way. A little less haste would lead to much more progress.

There are clearly shortcomings in mathematical achievement and these are sometimes wrongly ascribed to curriculum changes in the direction of what is, out of ignorance, called modern mathematics. Such changes have actually come about to broaden the curriculum and correct the over-emphasis on mechanical arithmetic, often at the behest of the Inspectorate. But this broadening and improvement is unlikely to happen so long as there is an emphasis on getting things *right*, rather than concentrating on the understanding of the child. Learning mathematics is not about getting lots of ticks in exercise books. It is about children gaining understanding, and through that the power to operate fully with mathematical concepts which they can apply in the real world. Such problem-solving approaches might take more time to work out, but the child who has done this will have a deeper understanding, a relational understanding, which will not need constant revision in order to be remembered. We have to ask ourselves: 'Can instrumental understanding ever be enough?' If the answer is 'No', then we must insist that children are given the basis for a proper mathematical education in all our schools.

8 | Educating scientists

Teach your scholar to observe the phenomenon of nature; you will soon rouse his curiosity, but if you would have it grow, do not be in too great a hurry to satisfy this curiosity. Put the problems before him and let him solve them himself . . . Let him not be taught science, let him discover it . . . If you ever substitute authority for reason he will cease to reason; he will become a mere plaything of other people's thoughts. (*Emile*, J.J. Rousseau)

This quotation is used in the introduction to *Science for the Under-Thirteens*, a booklet produced by The Association for Science Education in 1971. Scientific investigation begins with close observation of phenomena, and this is so whether the scientist is a PhD student or a four-year-old. Very young children will sometimes be able to put forward a hypothesis to account for what they have observed. The following is an extract from a recorded discussion between two four-year-olds and their nursery teacher. A group of children from the class had been taken to the fishmonger's to buy a fish, which the teacher then cut up for them to look at. They had already discussed the function of the gills and the fact that people can't live in water, while fish can't live out of it:

Teacher: Shall we try the eye? Look!
Child 1: You cut it out.
Child 2: Get it out.
Teacher: Take the cover off
Child 1: Why?
Teacher: And look, would you like to see it?
Child 1: No I wouldn't. I think it's sharp in the eye, I do.
Teacher: Is that like our eye?
Child 1: No.

Teacher: In what way is it different?
Child 1: It's got plastic on.
Child 2: And it hasn't got any eyebrows.
Child 1: And we haven't got plastic over our eyes, have we?
Teacher: Why would a fish have plastic over its eye and we haven't?
Child 1: To keep its eyes not watery.

These young children, with the help of their teacher, were conducting a scientific investigation and attempting to account for the phenomena they observed. At this stage it is not important whether or not the product (their hypothesis) is correct, what is important is that they are learning to look closely and to think about the function of what they see, discuss their ideas, and make guesses. Science does not necessarily require large laboratories and complicated paraphernalia. In an article in *The Guardian* (12 August 1986), David Womack suggested that science organised on a vast scale had its limitations, and put forward various topics ideally suited to individual scientific investigation. He wrote that the main ingredients to success are not qualifications and expertise, but imaginative experimental design coupled with meticulous and sensitive observation, and quoted the example of the Austrian zoologist Karl von Frisch, who earned a Nobel Prize for his discovery in the 1940s of the 'language' of the bees. He used only the simplest of home-made apparatus to prove that foraging honey bees convey information about food sources through distinctive dances:

> So don't wait until you've saved enough money for your own personal cyclotron; you need look no further than your backyard for a laboratory. If you think you notice an unusual effect, follow it up directly with an experiment to test your informed hunch, and continue until you are certain in your own mind that a causal link exists. Scientific confirmation can come later when others check your findings using more sophisticated laboratory facilities.

The idea that science teaching in school ought to be the learning of immense stores of facts and formulae is one which has been criticised by many scientists. If minds are stuffed with out-of-date details, is this really the best preparation for a scientific career?

Wouldn't it be more useful for schools to prepare students by giving them more opportunities to conduct experiments, apply scientific method and retain open minds?

In his book *The Structure of Scientific Revolutions*, Thomas Kuhn, the American physicist, wrote that a crisis arose in a science when new data caused contradictions which could not be resolved without changing the ways of thinking then current. Contemporary scientists would be aware only that something had gone fundamentally wrong at a level with which their training had not equipped them to deal.

He goes on to assert out that almost always those who achieved the fundamental inventions of a new paradigm were either very young or very new to the field. They were so little committed by prior practice to traditional rules of normal science that they were more likely to see that those rules no longer defined a playable game, and so were able to conceive another set to replace them.

The heuristic method

This term means finding out, encouraging the desire to find out; it is the art of discovery in logic and, applied to education, describes the method by which pupils are set to find things out for themselves. It is the method advocated by Comenius and Rousseau. In England, the statesman Edmund Burke wrote in the 18th century:

> I am convinced that the method of teaching which approaches most nearly to the methods of investigation is incomparably the best.

John Dewey, writing in the 19th century, made the point that textbooks were offered as a substitute for the child's present, active life. Material introduced by textbooks which had no connection with the child's experience made the material formal and symbolic (at a stage in the child's life when it was not yet thinking in the symbolic mode). In its genuine form, a real symbol served as a factor in the holding of a truth in the mind, but a symbol introduced from outside was dead and barren.

In *The Child and the Curriculum*, Dewey wrote:

> Even most scientific matter, logically arranged, loses this quality by the time it reaches the child, when presented in an external

fashion. Thought-provoking characteristics are lost and it becomes stuff for memory. Thus the child gets neither the advantage of the adult logical formulation, nor of his own apprehension and response. Hence the logic of the child is hampered and mortified and he gets degenerate reminiscence, second- or third-hand experience.

In England at the turn of the century, Professor Henry Armstrong, Professor of Chemistry at London University, was dissatisfied with the attainments of chemistry students at the City & Guilds of London Institute for the Advancement of Technical Education, and ascribed their shortcomings to defects in school-teaching methods. He found that teachers told pupils too much and allowed them to do few experiments by themselves. Excessive reliance was placed on verbal formulations and on textbooks; the spirit of enquiry essential to science was absent.

To correct these defects, Armstrong, together with some of his colleagues, developed schemes of teaching and these were adopted, after 1900, by many schools, especially in London. The subject of chemistry was presented as a series of simple research problems within the capacity of children. Instead of being told the properties and chemical name of chalk, children were given lumps and asked to find its chemical composition, while the teacher restricted himself to hints and minimum directions about the experiment to be performed by pupils. This led to school laboratories being built according to Armstrong's directions, so that it was difficult for teachers to lecture or show children experiments.

The criticisms made by orthodox teachers were that the heuristic, or discovery, method led to slow acquisition of factual knowledge and penalised students in public examinations, and that they were artificial since students only looked things up in textbooks, instead of making the investigations themselves. The first criticism is still made today, but it rather misses the point, which is that the amassing of a vast store of factual knowledge cannot be speeded up if it is to be understood and applied. The second one must depend upon the kind of early training those students had received. In many ways these arguments reflect Richard Skemp's thesis on relational and instrumental understanding. In order to apply one's knowledge and develop original work, one needs relational understanding. In order to pass public examinations, and do routine work, one can manage with instrumental understanding.

Nevertheless it became generally admitted in the early years of the century that science teaching should always be permeated by a heuristic basis, and methods of investigation must be used wherever possible. Yet when HMI published the report *Primary Education in England* in 1978, they found only 5 per cent of teachers using mainly exploratory methods, while 75 per cent used mainly didactic methods of teaching. Twenty per cent used a combination of methods. They wrote:

> In most classes the content of children's work and their use of resources is so prescribed, sometimes to the extent that there is insufficient opportunity for the children to incorporate information and ideas of their own or to make use of spontaneous incidents which arose.

They found that teachers had difficulty in selecting and using subject matter, especially in science *where no individual item of experimental work was to be found in 80 per cent of the classes for any age* (my emphasis). If we are short of mature scientists, perhaps we must look to the primary schools which do not encourage the necessary exploratory work, and to the secondary schools in which teaching is still largely didactic.

The HMI report did not distinguish between different local education authorities, but it would have been interesting had it done so, for I would hazard a guess that there is more exploratory work done in primary schools in London than in some other parts of the country. The reasons for this are, first, that the ILEA and its own inspectorate and advisory staff encourage this approach, and run courses to this end; secondly, that the ILEA schools are still better resourced than most schools elsewhere in the country. In recent visits to 50 or 60 schools in the ILEA area I have been impressed by the efforts being made to develop scientific investigation and method in many of them.

What the children are actually doing

Children in nursery classes have fish, animals and growing plants to observe and handle. A surprising number of children in this age group are able to produce striking and closely-observed drawings and even paintings of the plants and animals, to note the animals' habits and describe them orally to their teachers. They are able to use magnifiers, and even make informal measurements of plant growth, using pieces of string, marks on sticks, or their own handspans. There is weather observation – a constant topic in Britain. They are investigating and reflecting on the properties of sand and water, and discussing their findings with their fellow pupils, their teachers, and other adults. They are making dough and baking cakes, and observing and discussing the chemical changes caused by heat. Insects are studied. There are simple books on relevant subjects available for them to look at. There is conversation with other children and adults about comparative weights, sizes and colours of everything around them. There is education on health, care of teeth and bodies, toilet habits, food values and suitable clothing.

In most infant classes, where this work is developed, children begin to record their observations in a variety of ways, from picture diagrams to block graphs. I have seen the most detailed drawings of the transformation of tadpoles into frogs, done with the aid of magnifiers, accompanied by meticulous descriptions of the process in self-made books. Magnets are a source of useful investigative work, discovering the set of things which are attracted by the magnet, and the set of things which are not so attracted, and finding out why. And as the children become more competent readers, the books available in the classroom are a resource for confirming what has been discovered. Sometimes explanations will be provided by books, because no-one advocating this method of work believes that every child can in each case rediscover all this information by first-hand research. But so long as the recourse to books comes *after* the child has some first-hand experience, he or she can build what is grasped from the book into the mental structure which has developed from the first-hand experience. Learning involves the marriage of theory and practice.

Investigation of food values can be extended and different substances can be tasted and compared. A study of the human body and its workings – with, for example, the children comparing themselves as babies with their present physiques – involves the working out of similarities and differences. Investigation of the process of growth; observational work on skeletons, both animal and human; the study of living creatures: all are subjects of intense fascination for young children. So too are mechanical and electrical topics, experiments with batteries, wheels and pulleys. Further, it is mistaken to think that only boys are interested in such topics. I have seen both sexes fully involved, in classrooms where the assumption is that both boys and girls will be equally interested and are equally competent in these areas.

Everything in the children's environment can be investigated, examined, and used to establish a basic scientific approach which not only encourages their curiosity, but enables them to tackle investigation in a systematic way. As they mature and their skills increase they are able to record more and more, and in this way they also receive the opportunity to practise those basic skills appropriately and purposefully. A child cannot make a scientific examination without using language, and most require the application of some mathematical skills as well.

The following is reproduced from an infant shared book, that is to say a book made by a group of under-seven-year-olds, with captions either written by children or dictated to the teacher. The children had had an incubator in the school and had been observing the emergence of chickens:

Page 1. This is the six chicks.
2. Chicks come out of eggs. They peck the shell open and push it apart with their legs and back.
3. Chicks are small and sticky and pink when they hatch.
4. They are very weak at first and they keep falling over.
5. When the stickiness dries off, the chicks are covered with soft, furry down, all yellow and cream.
6. The chicks have got very little wings with tiny feathers on them. The wings grow quickly.
7. Chicks' legs are long, pink and skinny.
8. Chicks' feet have three long toes pointing forwards and one toe at the back. They have long claws for scratching in the earth.
9. Chicks have sharp pink beaks to peck at their food.
10. Chicks' ears are little round holes near to their eyes. When their feathers grow their ears are hidden.
11. A new dry chick weighs 61 grammes, that's the same as 4 pairs of scissors or 16 crayons or 11 marbles.
12. New chicks are 11 cm tall, that's as tall as a stick of glue.
13. They are 7 cm long. A wax crayon is 7 cm long.

This is a record of a detailed investigation in which the children developed their powers of observation, their descriptive language, and carried out the weighing and measuring.

In an article *Does content matter in primary science?*, Wynn Harlen, who played an important part in developing an innovative science curriculum, wrote:

> Many early ideas are incomplete or ill-defined and later have to be modified and refined as children's experience widens. It is this gradual change towards ideas of greater applicability and generalisability that constitutes their progress. Thus one should expect somewhat different ideas in relation to particular phenomena or explanations from a nine-year-old or an 11-year-old. (*School Science Review* June 1978)

This modification and refinement can be found in children's work and ideas as they move up through the primary school. Below is the account by a ten-year-old studying a stick insect through a microscope:

> The antenna is quite long and the colour is greenish brown and it has little bits of the hair along the sides. It is made in segments and can bend like our back. If you touch the antenna the stick insect jerks away. The colours of the eye are black and white. It is made up in the same way as a bee's eye. Through the microscope I could see it was made up of hexagons and each of these is an eye, so if I look at the insect it will see about a hundred pictures of me.
>
> I soon focussed the foot and I could see the claws. They are quite sharp and are used to keep a grip on the branches. I turned the insect over and soon had a focus on the sucker, it looks jellyish and is used as an anchor if the claws lose grip.
>
> The mandibles – I got a focus on them and there was a dark colour behind them. So I lowered the lens and there I saw the two halves of the mouth and in a close up they looked horrible.
>
> The joint in the leg – I got a very good focus on the joint with the 6X and it looked as if it was made of rubber, it has to be stretchy for the movement it does.
>
> I got a focus of the (wing) cases with the 10X lens and I thought the veins looked like the veins in a leaf. Then I saw a brown

spot and I thought it was either a burn or an illness the insect died of.

The greater sophistication of the ten-year-old is quite clear in a comparison of these two observational accounts. I do not know whether the reference to the bee's eye arose from a previous investigation, or from seeing an illustration in a book. But this child was clearly capable of making use of information from books – he was moving towards the symbolic stage – but his motivation arose through curiosity and his current work was developed on the basis of earlier exploration and investigation. He had also spent considerable time previously observing the behaviour of stick insects and drawing them.

The importance of content

Although I think primary science should be mainly concerned with process and investigation, I believe that the content should never be trivial. Children are interested in significant problems which they come across; part of the teacher's task is to present these in ways which the child can investigate successfully. The teacher also has objectives in terms of the general principles which he or she wants the child to begin to perceive. Wynn Harlen wrote:

> While children are investigating problems they find, and developing scientific skills and attitudes, what is the core of generalisations that they should at the same time acquire?
>
> The words *at the same time* cannot be emphasised too much. The content objectives must not be allowed to replace the process and attitude objectives. So it is perhaps necessary to state explicitly that our central concern in primary science should be to develop the abilities to:
>
> Observe, raise questions, propose enquiries to answer questions, experiment or investigate, find patterns in observations, reason systematically and logically, communicate findings, apply learning.
>
> And the attitudes of:
>
> Curiosity, originality, co-operation, perseverance, open-mindedness, self-criticism, responsibility, independence in thinking.

The development of these abilities and attitudes, rather than the conducting of a list of set experiments, should be the aim of the primary teacher, and many local education authorities have produced guidelines which are used as a basis for such scientific work. But this work in science should not be restricted to guidelines, because many useful areas for study arise fortuitously, out of other work that children may be involved in. This highlights one of the problems of having a centralised curriculum: because something that has become of burning interest to a child or group of children is not specified in the guidelines, this fact can serve as a justification for restricting the range of enquiry. This would be a retrogressive step because there are differences of interest arising out of different local environments, and the encouragement of such enquiries can lead to the most valuable learning.

9 | Art, music and movement, and all that jazz

Primitive man decorated the walls of his cave with pictures, which he made by using tools. Whatever other significance these paintings had for him, they were an art form. 'The hand is the cutting edge of the mind' said Jacob Bronowski in *The Ascent of Man*.

Children do not draw or paint mindlessly. There is an inherent satisfaction in creating art in any medium, and in viewing works of art of all kinds. In the learning process the movement of the hand becomes more refined, and the eye becomes better able to focus. So drawing, painting, modelling, clay work and printing are all of importance both for the child's own development, and also because they are an important starting point for the development of other communication skills – speech, reading and writing. Experience in using different sizes of paper and in placing marks in the space of the paper, for example, also assists the development of children's spatial concepts. Close observational work increases awareness and develops the ability to notice minute differences, an attribute which proves valuable in many areas of study. It also demands of the artist that the work correlate with reality.

A work of art, in any medium, requires a child to make decisions about materials, form, colour and position and these provide opportunities for the necessary practice in decision making, thereby developing judgement in the learner. The very skills which are developed in this way often seem to correlate with the development of reading and writing skills. There may be some learning overlap; hand-eye co-ordination may be refined, with a consequent improvement in the hand control needed for writing, or perhaps the cathartic effect of art work frees the child emotionally to concentrate on those other skills.

The universality of early art

In *Pre-school and Infant Art*, Kenneth Jameson, former ILEA Inspector for Art, wrote:

> From world-wide studies of young children's art, it is clear that there are patterns of development which are universal. They apply in Africa, Japan, Tonga, Austria or England . . . These patterns of development are clearly seen in the content of the children's work, in the universality of the symbols they use and the order in which they use them, both of which aspects are surprisingly constant.

Kenneth Jameson describes how children everywhere begin by scribbling with their fingers in their food, in sand, on steamy windows. They will use chalks, pencils, crayons and paint on paper or any other material, when these are provided. Gradually they gain control 'until they acquire the power to repeat certain marks and signs and shapes' and the emerging form is a movement towards the oval. This oval symbol is repeated and is called variously 'cat', 'house', 'mother', 'me', 'face'. This can happen anywhere between the ages of two-and-a-half and five-and-a-half. Gradually this symbol is developed with lines and dots and becomes a figure more recognisable to adults and it begins to stabilise in the mind of the child. Kenneth Jameson also writes about children's use of patches of colour when they are painting, rather than drawing with paint. When the child has moved through these two developmental patterns 'the stage is set for growth and development in the light of experience'.

In a useful booklet, *Some Functions of Art in the Primary School*, another two ILEA Art Inspectors, Mary Newland and Maurice Rubens, write about the importance of children learning to look: 'Looking absorbs, engages, calms and sensitises the learner.' In some way art work can help children to shake off serious problems and free them to establish more control over themselves, a necessary prerequisite for gaining more control over the outside world.

The story of David

When I was teaching a class of six-year-olds, many years back, a small boy, David, was brought to join the class in mid-term. He had come to live in a local children's home having been rejected by prospective adoptive parents. This had happened after various other unhappy experiences in his short life. He was a very disturbed little boy who spent his time disturbing others – understandably. Nevertheless, as the teacher, I had to protect other children from him, and protect him too, from himself, because he would demonstrate his feelings of guilt and self-dislike by trying to punish himself physically. I managed to involve him in painting, but he would almost always finish by covering his paintings in thick scribbles of black or brown paint.

I had been in the habit of bringing in prints which we would look at and discuss, and I would mount these in a low position on the classroom wall so that the children could view them closely if they wished. One day I brought in a Vermeer print called *The Music Lesson*. After our critical session I put it on the wall, and David immediately stationed himself in front of it and examined it very closely. Shortly afterwards he came and asked if he could do a painting of the print. We moved an easel near the painting, and he began to copy the print. He spent a long, long time on the work, and when he had finished, his copy was much admired by the other children and by me. We put his picture up beside the print. For the next few days he copied this print obsessively and his copies were carefully treasured by being turned into a large book, titled *David's Book of Vermeer*.

What was especially notable about this? These were the first paintings of his that David did not wish to obscure with black or brown paint scribbles. His copies were interesting in themselves, as pictures painted by a six-year-old, and he derived pride and joy from painting them, two emotions which had been in short supply in his life hitherto. The admiration of his peers enabled him to establish better relationships than he had done previously; he felt on more of an equal footing and did not have to resort to aggression. He became altogether *calmer* and more reasonable, and he began to learn to read, which he had not been able to do before.

David left the area soon after this, going again for a trial adoption, and I moved to another school. I made enquiries about his welfare but never found out how he had got on in his new home. Of one thing I am sure, his experience with paint while copying the Vermeer was the most positive thing that had happened for him in school. I don't know why that particular painting should have had that effect, except that it does have a very calm atmosphere, common to Dutch interiors. But the reasons why are unimportant; the important thing is that works of art can be vitally important in our lives and young children *need* to be given opportunities to experience them.

Drawing to learn

To draw is primarily a gestural, ordering, act.

Drawing keeps the eye engaged and is an excellent starting point in deciphering an unfamiliar object visually.

The pencil's purpose is not to 'Teach Drawing', its purpose is to hold the child longer in the presence, to prolong the period of attentive looking and to allow time to relate what is known, told or seen. New ideas are promoted leading to greater understanding. (*Some Functions of Art in the Primary School*)

Drawing and painting involve a child in both thought and movement; the large, sweeping arm movements and smaller precise movements all assist children to develop co-ordination. Body movement of all kinds is vital to children's development.

First movement, then thought

Life begins with movement. The ultimate uniting of sperm and egg is dependent upon movement. During pre-natal development, embryo and foetus are in constant motion as cell division and gradual differentiation prepare a new life for birth – movement into the world. This movement from a state of complete dependence to a state of relative independence requires rapid adjustments. The urge to survive forces the infant to move. He must eat, breathe, excrete . . .

Body movement is being actively recognised as an underlying and essential component in children's learning . . .

Through body movement the child discovers consistencies which in turn create patterns of response – knowledge in the making . . . On the outside he merely seeks to cope; inwardly he is organising his perceptions of the world. (*Moving and Knowing*, Lydia A. Gerhardt)

There is a clear link between movement and conceptualisation. The infant, waving its hands in the air, kicking its feet, raising its head, learning to roll, crawl and, finally, walk, is constantly interacting with its environment and developing concepts about space and time. Human beings are designed to move and without movement there can be no healthy growth. While there is an awareness of the need for movement or exercise for physical health, there is less recognition of the importance of movement for cognitive development. In fact children are told not to 'fidget'. 'Sitting still' is thought by many to be a prerequisite for concentration, while observation indicates that the converse may be much more likely.

In a study of mathematical ability in schoolchildren in the USSR, *The Psychology of Mathematical Abilities in Schoolchildren*, V.A. Krutetskii, a Soviet psychologist, observed repeatedly that gifted children did not sit still. He writes, for example, about Sonia, aged eight:

> She is capable of deep concentration. When she is concentrating she does not sit quietly but moves around, fidgeting, sometimes even assuming unnatural poses. Once, while studying a hard problem . . . at her home, to our amazement she got up unexpectedly, went to the bed, turned a somersault in a businesslike way, and returned to her chair.

Of Lenya he notes:

> At seven, Lenya knew how to write, count and read. Seven year-old Lenya was a very active boy. He was not able to sit still for five minutes – he would get up, run around the room, fidget and jump. He did problems while fidgeting and moving incessantly. The impression was that it helped him. His mother once jokingly remarked: 'I think that if he were tied down he would not be able to solve a problem!'

Thus, having accepted the natural, inborn need for movement in children, what role should the school have? First, there must be space for children to move about in classrooms and an understanding of their compulsion to do so. The school curriculum must provide ample opportunities for children to utilise their impetus to movement and develop their spatial concepts. Quite a lot of work in mathematics can be undertaken with the children themselves acting as units – when making sets, for example, or in describing angles of turn. Physical education periods can be linked with mathematical work, in shape-making or reflection – where children in pairs try to reflect their partners' movements. This is not work done with body alone – if there is such a thing – it is work in which the child's mind is fully engaged. Ball games also require developed space-time concepts and hand-eye co-ordination.

Moving to music

As well as moving about in the womb, it is now accepted that the foetus becomes accustomed to sound, and 'womb music' is available commercially, to lull babies to sleep with familiar, security-imparting sounds. Very young babies listen to music. Children use their voices and bodies rhythmically in their play, and clapping is an early accomplishment:

> As an organisation of sounds in time, music making reflects body control as well as thinking. It is through body movement that the young child can organise his musical thinking. Rhythm melody, and dynamics in music are 'sensed' through body movement. Clapping, hopping, skipping, or galloping reflect a sense of rhythm; when these activities are accompanied by music, the child can further clarify his musical ideas about rhythm, tempo, and dynamics. As the child develops control of his movement, he can express such musical concepts as melody. The movement of his body can express the shape, length and direction of melody as well as the changing intensities of the beat. Spatial ideas can be explored through experiences with rhythm, melody and tempo, as music embodies points of reference balance, time . . . direction, distance/length and volume. (*Moving and Knowing*)

Clearly music and movement and dance are aspects of the school curriculum which are important both in themselves and for their role in the development of children's concepts of time and space and in the understanding of their own bodies. And perhaps in learning the dances of other cultures, children learn more from them than merely the dance steps and rhythms – another important result could be a growth in respect for other peoples and their cultures.

What is a frill?

Intertwined with the cries of 'back to the basics' there has often been the accusation that there is too much time spent on 'frills' such as art and music. In many LEAs the teaching of instrumental music has been taken out of the school curriculum for reasons of economy, and justified in terms of more time needing to be spent on those 'basics'. What does this mean in real terms to the children in those areas? That musical talent can only be developed in the children of those well off enough to pay for private music lessons? Throughout the country there must be hundreds of thousands of children whose parents cannot pay – the children of the unemployed and those in low-paid jobs. These children are being denied an opportunity to develop skills which could determine their future careers and would certainly enrich their whole lives.

Like art, music can become a key in unlocking a child's ability to learn. I remember a nine-year-old who seemed unable to concentrate on learning, either at home or at school; his greatest satisfaction seemed to come from disturbing his classmates. Then an opportunity arose for him to learn to play the cello. Unlikely as it may seem, he made real progress with the instrument, became much calmer and, as he gained control over the cello, seemed to gain control over himself. He changed considerably in his behaviour and made more progress with his studies. Whatever the cost of his lessons, they were much less than would have been the cost of sending him into special education for the maladjusted, which would otherwise probably have been necessary.

Another important area for young children is drama. Children gain enormous enjoyment both from performing and from watching, and this is important in itself. Anna Scher and Charles Verrall, who run a children's theatre in north London, stress this:

> First and above all – enjoyment. Then comes a wide range of other benefits: it provides an outlet for self expression and helps the development of imagination and artistic awareness; it increases social awareness (particularly through role play), mental awareness, fluency of speech, self-knowledge, self-respect, self-discipline and self-confidence. It gives children the opportunity to learn how to co-operate with others and helps develop orderly thinking and the ability to organise. It improves physical co-ordination and physical fitness. It may also have a therapeutic effect, through helping children to deal with their real-life problems, or a cathartic effect, by enabling them to act out violence and frustration. It provides social and moral

training, and helps young people to mature emotionally, preparing them for adult life. (*100+ Ideas for Drama*)

There are two kinds of drama developed in school: the informal and the formal. Informal drama gives children the opportunity to act out problems and worries; it involves role play, and ideas are formed through discussion with the teacher and in the group. It is not meant for a wider audience although a theme can sometimes be developed and turned into something suitable for a public performance, but essentially this informal drama is a learning situation for all concerned.

Those children who enjoy performing (and not all children do) will often like to work towards something more formal, a performance for other classes in the school, or, even more ambitious, a performance for parents and friends, which requires the learning of words and the making of costumes and scenery, thus providing outlets for non-performers as well.

Both kinds of drama are important to a school, and there should be room for both, but informal drama is the most important for the children's intellectual and emotional development.

There are numerous companies of young actors and dancers, known as Theatre in Education and Dance in Education, storytellers and musicians who perform in schools, for a small fee. While inevitably standards vary, good groups perform an immensely valuable function by introducing young children to the professional theatre. The sight of small children's faces when they are held enthralled by the drama or the dance, seen at close quarters, is most moving. Some groups choose their themes carefully and liaise with schools about their projected play. Notes are prepared for teachers, and both preparatory and follow-up work can be carried out. During performances the child audience is often involved as judge or jury, and can affect the play's direction. Issues important to the children – friendship, jealousy, loss of parents, loneliness, the effects of prejudice, racism and sexism – can be portrayed in a way which stimulates children's thinking, without telling them what they should think. The acting out of situations with which children can empathise can also be most helpful for children affected by such sadnesses.

Unhappily, many of these companies have been affected by financial cuts, both in their own subsidies and in the sums which schools have to spend on such entertainment for the children.

Schools which cannot afford to buy books will hardly be able to raise the money to engage a theatre company. Many of these talented youngsters have had to join the ranks of the unemployed, and the schools have suffered.

When doors are being closed in this way the young unemployed may be the worst affected but in the long run we all lose by this restriction of opportunity. The loss of outlets for creativity can lead to immense frustration and the kind of despairing violence we have seen too often. It is a tragedy that this is happening when what is needed is an expansion in adult education and funding for drama, music and craft groups, so that young people can develop their potential and produce art, drama and craft work which will enrich both their own lives and the lives of others – especially, as we have seen, in primary schools.

And the schools themselves need a broad arts curriculum which gives pupils the opportunity to experiment with different forms of expression. This is not a matter of frivolity. As the 1982 Gulbenkian Report, *The Arts in Schools*, pointed out:

> Creative work is not merely a question of playing with things, of randomness and chance. It has much to do with serious and sustained effort, often at the highest levels of absorption and intensity.
>
> This involves respect for standards and aiming purposefully, often at great expense of time and effort, and producing works of high quality.

Parents and teachers should put the utmost pressure on the government to ensure that the resources going into schools are not only for new technology to be introduced, but also to protect and extend children's artistic opportunities. Our children need to develop as whole people, and their emotional and artistic needs are ignored at society's peril.

10 | Breaking new ground

There are some relatively new areas in the primary curriculum which I feel need mention here, and there is also now more of an inter-disciplinary approach which may be unfamiliar to many parents reared on compartmentalised subjects like geography and history. The latter is best explained by a look at environmental studies.

Looking at the neighbourhood

Many primary schools take children out into their own neighbourhood and organise a study which spans several disciplines. The study will be concerned both with the local geography, making maps of the area, routes to school, and so on, and with the history, which can be discovered through investigation and research. Such a study will also draw on mathematics, geology, commerce and economics, sociology, scientific research, architecture, building technology, sanitation and transport facilities. Local industries may be studied – which could lead children into research into chemistry, metallurgy, food technology, and so on.

A study of the local environment, beginning with what children already know, does not necessarily remain limited to the locality, because links with the world at large will be discovered through transport, through postal services, through foreign imports to be found in local shops. The interest aroused by such links can be developed in many ways which will extend the children's knowledge and understanding of the world.

Many skills are used in such studies. The children will photograph, draw and paint what they see. They will write factual descriptions and imaginative accounts of features of the area. They may find themselves estimating and measuring distances; timing journeys by foot, bicycle, bus, train or car; traffic counts may be taken at various sites. They will learn techniques of interviewing and recording what they are told; they may learn to use film and tape for their recording.

I have seen an excellent environmental project in which the degree of pollution was measured in the school playground, in the road outside the school and in the local park. This led to the collection and weighing of litter, the investigation of litter and a much higher consciousness of its dangers to the environment, as well as some outstanding art work using a variety of junk materials collected from local industries. It also led to a project to transform the school playgrounds and make them more attractive and social areas for children.

In work of this kind, the introduction of computers into the schools has been a useful addition to school resources.

Computer whizzkids

By taking the drudgery out of the compilation of statistics, the use of the computer is an effective tool in projects like the one described above. This is probably the area of work with the most educational potential, where children – who very quickly learn how to operate these machines – can put in their own data and use programs to restructure the information and so gain new insights. There have been some excellent projects reported in teaching journals. One involved a class investigation of the history of the area around a school, using published census reports. It enabled the children to learn a great deal about the uses of the computer as a machine, and techniques for the organisation and extrapolation of data. But they also learned about the history of the area where they lived: the actual work being done was of value in itself and would have been a fascinating and worthwhile project if it had been done without using the computer. With the computer much of the mechanical drudgery was eliminated and the children were able to concentrate on the content of their project.

By using the computer for research, children will begin to understand what it is and what it can do. For some the computer will simply remain an excellent tool. But there will be those who become fascinated by the electronic wizardry and who will want to pursue technical investigations of the computer itself. Judging by the problems I have encountered working with a word processor, it is clear that I do not qualify for the title of this section. But many youngsters whom I have met in schools do. The technology with which we grow up is something we take for granted; I know of one teenager who is called in by his teachers when there is a problem on a computer, because he is always able to solve all the difficulties which arise. Some girls and boys seem to have a very rapid grasp of the possibilities and limitations of the computer, and gain a mastery and skill which promises to develop far beyond that of their teachers. Some talented older children will be able to produce programs for younger children to use. Or someone who has overcome a reading or mathematical difficulty through use of the computer might well be able to devise programs to help others with similar difficulties.

The computer has many advantages in remedial work because computing is very much a high-status occupation in the classroom and competency in this area could build up the confidence of those who do not have a good self-image. For children who have experienced reading difficulties, the computer offers the advantage of working in what seems to be a fresh area, where the inhibitions arising from previous failures are less powerful. For the child with writing difficulties, the computer provides opportunities to produce legible communications, as does a typewriter, but with the advantage that he or she can make corrections, and still produce a perfect printout. So insofar as children are experiencing difficulties through a lack of self-confidence and a fear of making mistakes, a computer is a valuable tool. Just the necessity of reading the instructions can be, of itself, a motive for improving one's reading ability, where such a motive is lacking. The sense of being in control, that the computer operator has, is of the utmost value to an uncertain, insecure, learner.

A very positive aspect of computer work is the encouragement of collaborative work; it is common to see four, five or more children gathered around a computer, discussing and arguing. Hypotheses are put forward and debated, tested out; conclusions are drawn. In language work – for which some useful programs including word games and spelling checks have been produced – writing a story jointly often provides a needed stimulus and children strike creative sparks from one another. If the wrong spelling is pointed out briskly by other children and wiped out to be replaced by the correct one, it doesn't seem to carry the emotional overtones of correcting work under other circumstances, or at adult direction.

In the same way, mathematical exploration has the advantage that mistakes can be eliminated – without being marked wrong

– and several attempts made until solutions are found. There are many good mathematics programs – some of the best produced by teachers through local education authority organisations. Many of these present the user with problems in spatial relations, geometry and logic. Many commercial programs, however, are too mechanical, of too low a level and do not challenge the pupils' intellects sufficiently, so that they are merely games which, after being played, do not lead anywhere. Many involve arithmetical operations and are no more than a substitute for textbook practice, though they are more fun – but not for long, because they lack flexibility and soon become boring.

Valuable as work on the computer can be, it should never be seen as a substitute for first-hand practical experience. Drawing a cube on a computer is not the same as handling solid shapes, and it is questionable whether very young children should be introduced to work of this kind before they have sufficient first-hand experience. One useful device for young children is the electronic, computer-controlled module, the turtle. Experience with this can accelerate the development of spatial concepts, counting, appreciation of angles, and so on. It is a good and educative toy, but it should never replace the play with sand, water, bricks, Lego or clay, which is so important for children's development. But, used wisely, the variety of stimuli afforded by this medium is extremely wide, and, if well used, can develop children's thinking.

Young craftspeople, designers and technologists

This is an even more recent introduction, in formal terms, into primary schools than computing, although it has been promoted in secondary schools for some time, and informal work in the field has gone on in many primary classrooms for years. Jerome Bruner, in *The Process of Education*, wrote:

> There is an appropriate version of any skill or knowledge that may be imparted at whatever age one wishes to begin teaching – however preparatory the version may be. The choice of the earlier version is based upon what one is hoping to cumulate.

The aim is to make children more aware of design, more knowledgeable about modern technology, to increase craftwork in schools, and by combining these three fields, encourage exploration, creativity and inventiveness in our young children. Until quite recently, half our child population was never given the opportunity to develop skills in these areas – these were the girls who were largely confined to design and craft in textiles and cookery. They were not given opportunities to work with wood and metals. Of course, boys were also deprived of developing *their* skills in the fields thought to be female prerogatives, like sewing and cooking. More and more local education authorities are developing policies on equal opportunities so that all the school population can develop their talents in all these fields.

Because craft design and technology is a field where theory and practice are closely interwoven, it is a valuable addition to the primary school curriculum. Obviously primary school teachers will use the practical work for developing basic skills work too. Children will need to draw plans; having constructed a working model they might need to write out instructions for others. I think one of the most difficult tasks I was given as a nine-year-old was to write out the instructions for boiling an egg. I remember that I forgot to light the gas; someone else in the class forgot to put water into the saucepan, and practically everyone in the class left out at least one step. For children to have to organise their thoughts, work out all the steps, and put this into writing is a most valuable exercise, and one from which they will learn far more than they will from answering questions in a textbook.

This work will develop not only children's basic skills in language, but also in mathematics, and will link up closely with their scientific enquiry. The chief problem is to help large numbers of primary teachers to attend courses which will enable them to introduce the subject to their classes in a confident manner. A conference on higher education in London, in November 1986, was told by Eric Bolton – Senior Chief Inspector, HMI – that vacancies for mathematics and craft design and technology teachers in secondary schools had increased by 35 per cent between 1982 and 1986. (In the same period vacancies for physics staff had risen by 55 per cent.)

The other problem is that because it is a subject where academic work needs to be translated into the practical, it is an expensive subject, requiring a generous supply of construction materials, batteries and motors. While the so-called 'extravagant' authorities like the ILEA might be generous enough in their funding for schools in their area to be able to attempt this work, schools in those 'good' authorities who limit their spending so severely that even books and pencils are in short supply are not going to be able to find the resources to educate their children in this way.

If those groups who complain most about 'frills' in education, demanding that the curriculum be pared to its most basic, feel that computers and the materials for craft and design courses are too expensive for primary schools, let them reflect on those occasions when, wearing their other hats, they bemoan the fact that Britain is falling behind technologically. Could there be some connection between rigid economies and a lack of technological development?

Sex education

There has been much debate about the kind of sex education which there should be in secondary schools. Strong feelings have been expressed about the need for education about sex to be kept within a moral framework, though whose moral framework is not clear, since there cannot be said to be a morality to which everyone adheres. So what about sex education in the primary school?

I have always felt that sex education was an important part of parenting. I certainly preferred to discuss this, together with my husband, with our own children. Yet as a headteacher I was asked by parents to explain certain terms to children, and this I tried to do, if I was not able to persuade the parents themselves to discuss with their children the points that were worrying them.

In any case, I do believe that children's questions should always be answered truthfully, and there should, for young children, be access to books which offer information about conception and birth. There are some topics which, when being discussed with children, lead to questions about sex and child development being raised, and one hopes teachers would deal with these directly as they arise, in the same way as they would deal with questions on other areas of life.

Basically, sex education comes within the parameters of health education, which is a very wide area, and it forms part of the children's task of finding out about themselves. Since there are clear and obvious links between sex and marriage, and since marriage for many people is closely linked with religious and cultural customs, sex education can be discussed within those parameters as well. But the teacher can do no more than indicate the multiplicity of views which exist, many of them conflicting.

It is very difficult, if not impossible, for teachers to meet parental expectations when parents themselves have such different outlooks. There was an outcry recently about a book available in a London teachers' centre, *Jenny lives with Eric and Martin*, which describes the life of a child living with a homosexual father and his partner. Yet some children do live in such families: how can they be prevented from feeling victimised if their lifestyle is stigmatised as unwholesome? Many parents want the sanctity of marriage emphasised in sex education. But large numbers of children live in one-parent families, or with two parents who are not married to one another: that is the reality. Perhaps the only morality which could carry conviction with youngsters is that we are all members, one of another, and must make every effort not to inflict pain on anyone, but to develop caring relationships, both sexual and non-sexual.

Certainly teachers have a responsibility to the children they teach, as well as to the parents of the children. The recent publicity on child abuse and on AIDS make it clear that it is imperative that the young should have knowledge of how to protect themselves. If every child receives basic sex education in school, this must help. Those parents who feel they would prefer to discuss these questions with their own children will, of course, do so, but if they think about the dangers of ignorance in this context, they will also understand how important is the role of the school.

Some parents find it difficult to acknowledge their children's sexual development and worry that their sexuality will be stimulated by sex education. But ignorance of the facts and a lack of understanding of the changes in their own bodies are no protection against premature sexual experience, nor can they protect children against sexual attack and abuse. Such protection can only be gained through knowledge and understanding. Teachers can only discharge their responsibility to their pupils by ensuring that the children have access to information in this area as much as in any other part of the curriculum.

An idea that has gained currency is that homosexuality will be encouraged if it is taught about in a non-judgmental way. I know of no evidence for this, but a little investigation suggests that homosexuality *is* encouraged by single-sex institutions of all kinds, including single-sex schools. Yet I am not aware that there has ever been a suggestion that these institutions should be banned for this reason. Another mistaken belief is that because a teacher is homosexual, that teacher is a paedophile, or someone desirous of having sexual relations with children. Paedophiles do exist and should not be in any job which brings them into contact with young children. But many such people are heterosexual, yet we do not worry about heterosexual men teaching young girls, nor heterosexual women teaching young boys. Children need the knowledge that no adult, nor any other child, should make sexual overtures to them, and be able to act upon that knowledge. Children do need protection and that can be helped by sex education.

Media education – another way of looking at things

> The creation of a public opinion which counts because it is well informed on media issues is a matter of urgent necessity. (*Teaching the Media*, Len Masterman)

Very young children now come into contact with media technology. They can operate television sets and videos, radios and cameras. They are certainly an important section of the viewing public – both of photographs and films – and are in the radio and musical audiences. Some children come into school with more experience of television and video than of print. This has become an area in which the educational role of the school needs to be established. As Cary Bazalgette, a teacher-adviser in the education department of the British Film Institute, says in her introduction to *Picture Stories*, a BFI education booklet:

> I would argue that the aims of print literacy should be extended to all the media. In other words, I am saying that every medium can be thought of as a language. Every medium has its own ways of organising meaning, and we all learn to 'read' it, bringing our own understandings to it and extending our own experiences through it. This does not mean that the media are just neutral; that racism, sexism, violence, bias and all the ills the media get accused of, do not matter. They do matter: they matter in novels and plays and magazines and pamphlets too, but we do not hear arguments against reading on this account. We assume that the fully literate reader may be fully armed against them.

The visual images of photography, television, video and cinema are all very powerful, and especially so to young children, who may find it more difficult to sort out fact from fantasy. This makes it very important indeed that teachers exercise the same kind of judgement about the examples of these media forms as they do about the books they encourage their children to read. But this also applies to the printed word – different newspapers will give totally different slants to the same item of news: the medium and the message are interlocked. Cary Bazalgette also points out how every text is constructed:

> Almost everything in a media text is the result of choices. We chose the point size of the type in this booklet. The BBC chose Julia Somerville to read the news. Reasons can be found for these choices . . . Media education will thus encourage children to think, and ask about these choices, as in, 'who would have taken this picture, and why?'; and of course, in making their own choices.

By making children aware of media constructions, they will be able to consider how and why different meanings can be drawn from the same set of facts. They will also be able to be more conscious of their own motives when working with media, in whatever form – writing, photography, or cinema and television. Certainly they will be in a far better position to make intelligent critical judgements, which should, after all, be one of the main aims of primary education.

11 | Whatever is an integrated day?

One of the most irritating experiences we suffer is having to leave some task in which we are deeply involved before we have completed it. Imagine then the frustration experienced by a young learner who is on the verge of solving a problem, on the verge of *understanding*, when ordered by the teacher to pack up the work, hand it in, or leave it to be finished at another time. While it is not possible to eliminate this situation completely, since all our lives are constrained by time, it is possible to minimise these occasions in schools by using a more flexible approach.

Different schools and teachers find different solutions. Sometimes children have a list of tasks to be done in any one day, or in any one week, and these can be done in any order, so long as all are completed within the given time. The tasks will cover all the areas of the school curriculum and the teacher will be able to check the children's work at the end of that time.

Another way of working is to set group tasks which involve work in many areas of the curriculum: for example, a group might be asked to make a weather chart for a week. Included in their task might be the measurement of shadows in one spot at the same time each day and the drawing of a graph to illustrate this. They might be asked to monitor weather forecasts on television each day, check their accuracy, and work out a method of illustrating how accurate or inaccurate they were. They could devise means of determining wind direction and finding out whether this had any connection with rainfall. Part of their task could be to produce paintings to show the local landscape in sun and rain, and the composition of prose, poetry, music and dance, to convey the impact of various weather conditions. They could be asked to present their findings in writing and orally to the rest of the class. Thus a simple observational task would involve them in a good deal of scientific investigation, mathematical drawing, note taking and the verification of data gained, as well as its translation into language, art and music. All these things would not necessarily have to be asked for by the teacher: sometimes the children themselves will press for opportunities to extend the work – they might want to turn their ideas into movement, a play, or into a book.

While this work was going on there would not be one hour specially set apart for the mathematical work, nor would the art work be time-tabled for Tuesday between 2 and 3pm. Of course the teacher would monitor the progress, and might notice hesitation or indecision on the part of one child; that would be the time to suggest a new avenue, perhaps saying 'What about trying a painting of the storm clouds?' or 'Would you like to make a start on a rain gauge today?', as appropriate. But the day would not be chopped up into discrete periods for different subjects; there would be a continuous flow with one stage developing from another, and different sub-groups taking responsibility for different sections of the work. One responsibility the teacher has is to see that every child has opportunities to work in each area of experience, e.g. that A is involved in the music and poetry writing, as well as doing a share of the mathematical work, if A is someone who gets very involved with mathematical problems and might not contribute to other curriculum areas without a gentle reminder. Children involved in this work might become interested in one particular aspect e.g. meteorology, and wish to develop this further as a personal project, with help from teacher and parents. Or the group might then go on to constructing a barometer or weather vane – or move on to something quite different.

Thus the integrated day means there is a flow of work, interrupted only for essential breaks: hall time, for example – which has to be time-tabled and which, if it is not used punctually, would inconvenience other classes – and lunch time, although in the past children might often continue to work through part of their lunch times, and breaks too, if they were passionately involved in their task. But since this is something which usually involves the teacher being in the classroom as well, it has been restricted by the teachers' campaign in the recent past.

When a class is working in this way, there are advantages and disadvantages. Among the advantages are the following:
– Children can work at a task until it is completed to their satisfaction and can have enough time to achieve excellence.

– They can work at their own pace.
– They can more easily pursue a topic in which they are particularly interested.
– Since not all the children are writing or working at mathematics at the same time, the teacher can direct help where it is most needed.
– Children take a greater responsibility for their own learning and are more self-motivated.
– Because the classroom has to be organised so that children can help themselves to materials, they have plenty of legitimate reasons for movement, which they need during the course of their work, and which cannot be construed as 'fidgeting'.
– Because the classroom is so organised, the teacher is not occupied with low-grade tasks – such as giving out materials, cutting paper, supplying rulers – and is able to concentrate on asking questions which will stimulate the children into constructive areas for investigation, giving explanations when these are needed, and helping children carry out tasks which are beyond their ability to manage on their own.
– The children themselves can learn to organise the materials and equipment; younger children learn to read the labels which indicate where different equipment can be found. They learn to sort out the equipment and put it away in the right place: through sharing responsibility for the organisation of the room they become more responsible. They also learn to think about their room and make suggestions for improvements which can be tried out and acted on.
– Because of the way the class is working, the teacher needs, inevitably, to keep much more detailed records. (This also appears under disadvantages.)
– Because recording has to be more analytical it probably gives the teacher much more information about what each child understands than do more formal records.
– Since most real-life tasks involve the use of skills in more than one area, children perceive their tasks as more realistic and purposeful than practising skills through a textbook exercise for which the result is a series of ticks.
  The disadvantages are:
– The teacher has to put a great deal of thought and work into organising the classroom before the class comes into school.
– Rather than noting in the records that the class covered a topic such as averages, the teacher would record that some children,

A,B,C, and D, covered averages in the work they did, while children E to H were working on the angles of a triangle. He or she must then ensure that A to D cover the work on angles, while the second group tackles a problem dealing with averages. Clearly, this involves a teacher in more detailed record-keeping than a class taught as one unit.

– The teacher needs to monitor the work being done very carefully, to ensure that no-one in the class is missing out an area of experience which each child should encounter: this is done by observation and by study of the child's work record. Such study is more time-consuming than it would be if the class were working more formally.

I believe that the advantages of working in this way far outweigh the disadvantages.

Whole-class teaching

For some reason there seems to be an idea that one can never address the whole class if one is working in an integrated way. This is, of course, nonsense. There are many times when one can usefully work with a whole class, and story-telling is one of these times. A very useful way of organising reading is to have a set time, perhaps five minutes for the youngest children, increasing to 20 minutes for older classes, when everyone reads silently, for pleasure. There are times when it is desirable to introduce a new topic to the whole class, and there should be times when work which has been done by groups or individually is shown to the rest of the class, new information is shared, and discussion takes place.

There are times, when the class is working on a joint project, when a great deal of class teaching, exchanging of ideas, and sorting out of tasks will be necessary. The classroom is a workshop and the people working in it need to communicate with one another. Sometimes a meeting of everyone involved in the project is necessary, sometimes smaller discussions between groups or pairs have to go on.

At other times, there is need for a demonstration by a teacher, and it is more economical of time to do this before the whole class. Very often the attention of a whole class can usefully be drawn, there and then, to some special discovery or individual achievement. There is room for variety in the life of the classroom. Both children and teacher benefit from such variations. Children also learn that different behaviour, more self-control, is needed when one is part of a large group than when one is working in a small group.

Topics and projects

A topic is, in everyday language, something under discussion, or a subject under investigation, and the word is of course related to 'topical'. In schools, topic work is usually applied to individual work where children pursue an interest of their own. Partly because no teacher can be an expert in 20 or more different fields of enquiry, and partly because it is not physically possible to organise resources for so many disparate topics, it sadly often becomes no more than children copying from books, text and drawings, into their topic books. It need not be so; with parental help and skilled teaching, children can be stimulated to investigate or study their subject at first hand. Such topics as fashion or football, often suggested by children, can be turned into worthwhile studies when the students are spurred on to investigate the history and provenance of their subject. In fashion, the social functions of different fashions, the origins of materials used or the effect of the import of cotton on the Yorkshire woollen industry, can save the topic from triviality. So too, the study of how, where and when football first began can enlarge this topic. It is just in this way that children's immediate interests can be developed and extended. But this remains very demanding for a teacher who cannot possibly monitor individual work effectively on this scale.

A project, on the other hand, is a bigger undertaking involving a group, or more usually a whole class – sometimes a whole school or even a group of schools, co-operating and sharing the cost of expensive resources. I have experienced all these forms of project work and found them all worthwhile from the point of view of everyone involved. A project can last for as little as a week, with very young children, or a month, or a term. One project with which I was involved lasted a full year, and developments from it extended into the following year. In fact if a school project is to lead to a public exhibition of some kind, so that parents can see the results of their children's work, children and teachers need time in order to present that work to their own satisfaction, and a year is not too long for that level of endeavour. As with everything else in teaching, its success depends on several factors: on the teacher's enthusiasm, preparation, organisation and planning, and on the children's interest and involvement. Some projects originate with the teacher, others with the children, or with a child who fires others with his or her enthusiasm.

A project will have at its core the investigation of a problem, or an area of interest to the class. It might be something in the local environment that provides a worthwhile focus for research, a subject which arises spontaneously out of children's interests, or a subject which a teacher feels would repay thorough investigation – perhaps offering an opportunity to correct a curriculum weakness. A project should spread across many curriculum areas so that there will be mathematical and scientific investigations; opportunities for first-hand exploration and the gathering of facts; language development; opportunities for discussion and debate. Connected with it will be the possibilities of extending reading, the writing up of notes, imaginative writing, playwriting, drama and role play, art and craft work, the creation of music, and so on. It should increase children's understanding, and knowledge of the area being studied, introduce them to investigative techniques, give them opportunities to practise a variety of skills, and present their findings through many different modes of expression.

One infant class I taught became involved in a project in the following manner. One of the children, Peter, came into school one morning with a box of geological specimens he had found on a piece of waste ground where some houses had been demolished. There were about 20 different pieces of rock, and we looked at them, but I could not identify them. On our next visit to the local library we found some books which we could consult. Most of the children in the class were very interested in studying the rocks and trying to name them from the pictures in the books. Many of the children wrote about them and drew them. Our investigations involved us in learning about volcanoes, and interest in the moon led us to finding out about gravitational pull. As there was such a lot of interest in the origins of the rocks, I suggested to the children that we might visit the Geological Museum, and then arranged a visit for them. The museum offered a short lecture before we looked around, and I accepted this. With some interested mothers, and a student who was doing her observation in the class, we went off on our visit.

When we met our guide and lecturer, he was rather taken aback by the youth of his audience; although I had told the museum that this was a class of six- to seven-year-olds, this clearly had not impinged sufficiently until he saw them! However, they behaved impeccably and were fascinated by his talk. He handed around a section of meteorite, which we each held, and a small box of moon dust! We then showed him the rocks we had brought and he was able to identify some which we had not been able to do for ourselves. Armed with this fresh information we returned to school and were able to classify all the rocks which Peter had found. It was a project which had been of great interest and I hope some of those children maintained and developed the interest which was born then. But whether or not this happened, they learned a great deal about how to investigate, where to find information, and how to use a museum – all worthwhile objectives.

As well as this they had had ample opportunity to practise their basic skills in ways which they had found interesting. Some of them had managed to decipher some quite difficult information books (and not always the 'best' readers either) and everyone had produced a great deal of written work. They had weighed the rocks and made a graph of the results, drawn and painted them, compared how long they had been in existence (although this kind of time scale is not one which a teacher would normally introduce to infants, it was appropriate in this case because *they* were the ones who found the information and demanded to have it made clear). There was a lot of descriptive writing and the rocks also became the subject of imaginative stories, space stories and poetry. The work was finally publicly displayed as part of an exhibition at a local arts centre. Those children certainly learned the importance of mathematical, language and artistic skills in communication as they proudly conducted their parents and brothers and sisters around their display. As their teacher I learned that one can truly introduce any subject, at an appropriate level, to children of any age, just as Bruner has said (see chapter 7).

I have described a project which grew out of something spontaneous, the discovery of a box of rock specimens by a child. Three other projects, from different schools, which I would like to describe developed from different bases: one was a shorter project, lasting about a term, which began with an outing; another developed from a centre of interest suggested by the teacher and the last was much more complex, involved the co-operation of several schools, and led to a lot of public display of different kinds.

How awareness grows

The first project, which involved children in the age group 9-11, began with a visit to Kenwood House, at the edge of Hampstead Heath in London, where an exhibition had been arranged about the life of the builder of the house and his family. The project culminated with the performance of a dance drama in a local schools music festival. Here is an extract from some written work by three of the children who took part, followed by two of the poems written during the project, which were later printed in the school magazine:

The idea of slavery first began when we went on a visit to Kenwood House. . . The house was old and once belonged to a rich man called Lord Mansfield. He had a niece called Elizabeth. Elizabeth had a slave called Dido. Dido was the same age as Elizabeth. The two girls were the best of friends. In the house were lots of pictures of slaves. We couldn't believe people once owned people.

We drew pictures of our classmates dressed as slaves. . . The slaves were dressed in rich silks and satins. They wore turbans on their heads with dyed ostrich feathers sticking out.

Most people thought the slaves would be dressed in rags, but to our amazement they were dressed in fine clothes. I think the slaves were dressed elegantly because their owners wanted them to look clean and smart so they could boast to their friends that they were rich enough to let their slaves dress as nice as them.

The children from our class got very interested in this. When we went back to school we wrote poems about slavery. . . To get the idea of life on board ship in the 18th century we did a sort of drama.

The first poem printed below was set to music and became the theme in the dance drama which was performed at the music festival:

Many years ago

Many years ago, people owned people
Did you know? Did you know?
Wanted to be free like you and me

Did you know? Did you know?
Many tried
Many died
Many cried
Did you know?

Many years ago, ships came sailing
Did you know? Did you know?
To the shores of Africa
Did you know? Did you know?
Rich men bought
Rich men sold
New hides for old
Did you know?

Many years people dreamt of freedom
Did you know? Did you know?
Struggled to be free like you and me
Did you know? Did you know?
Many still try
Many still die
Many still cry
Did you ever realise?

Will we be free?

Sitting around our campfire at peace and at ease
Planning the rituals of tomorrow, our God we must please.
The hunt had been fruitful, meat we had some
But that night as we slept we did not know what was to come.
They were hiding in bushes, ten or twenty at least
And as they came tiptoeing our sleep had to cease
We struggled as they tied us up with strong rope
Some of us struggled so hard that the men could hardly cope
Climbing up the side of the ship and onto the deck
Once we sailed we had to scrub and clean every single speck
The journey was ended and we are taken out of the hold
They dragged us like animals to the market to be sold
For the rest of my life I worked just for me feed
Hoping for the day when my descendants will be freed.

These poems, and the other work produced, illustrate the depth
of the children's identification. The children were involved in map

work, looking at the territories from which slaves were kidnapped, the sea routes of the slave ships to the United States and the West Indies. Children in the class whose families came from African countries, and from the Caribbean, were able to express their feelings, and discussions about the immorality of slavery helped children to clarify their own views about racism and understand its origins in self-interest and prejudice. The class also considered the theme historically, which helped them to orientate themselves in time as well as space. Artwork and model-making were done, African prints and carvings collected and studied. This project developed out of a visit – it had not been planned for by the teacher ahead of time, but arose because the teacher responded to the children's keen interest in the subject, just as I myself had done in the other project described above.

Many teachers use a diagrammatic form to plan out their future work. These are called 'flow diagrams' because they show how a centre of interest is linked with different curriculum areas, and the teacher's objectives – the opportunities for learning that the children will have. Two project diagrams are shown on pages 132 – 3 and 136 – 7. One uses 'toys', a subject of interest to children of all ages, and shows how wide can be the ramifications of such a project with a class of infants. The other, 'canals', is an example of a project introduced by a group of teachers, in this case with invaluable help from a canal enthusiast, which grew to become a whole-school project and finally involved co-operation with other schools in the locality.

Toy project

The idea of a project on toys was discussed with a class of six- and seven-year-olds who responded with enthusiasm and promised to bring in toys of all descriptions. After discussion about the feasibility of this, it was agreed that their parents might feel concern at this prospect, and they decided that a letter home explaining the purpose of the toy collection would be a good idea. The children wrote the letters, with their teacher's help, and the teacher countersigned each one.

The next morning several toys were brought in, and a larger number of parents than usual came to ask the teacher about the project. Interest was keen, and the toy collection grew quickly. There was discussion about how the toys were to be sorted and displayed. Someone suggested 'girls'' and 'boys'' toys, but after consideration the class came to the conclusion that most toys were enjoyed by both sexes; boys in the class played with the dolls in the house corner and the girls were keen on woodwork and construction sets. The next suggestion was 'soft' and 'hard', and this was felt to be more useful. The teacher then asked which materials would be considered hard, which led the children to think about the different materials used. Eventually they decided to sort them by the chief material used in their composition. This led to five main groups: wooden toys, metal toys, plastic toys, soft toys, and paper toys (which included kites). Games, it was agreed, would have to be a separate category. Playing with the toys was also discussed, and, although everyone would want to try out the various toys, it was generally felt that the permission of the owner should be sought and given. A code of conduct for the treatment of toys was worked out, and two of the children volunteered to write it out for display. One clause which everyone was very definite about was that any trespass on the code would result in immediate loss of the privilege of playing with the toys.

The next task was the recording of ownership and provenance: Derek's electronic game had been a birthday present only two weeks earlier, while the rocking horse which Mandy's father had brought had been used by him when he was a child and was at least 30 years old. Four children were given the job of recording ownership and collecting as many details about each toy as were available. Another five children sorted the toys out into their appropriate sets, while five more arranged each set in its agreed display area, which meant quite a lot of classroom rearrangement, involving consultation with the teacher. Four more children were engaged in sorting out board games into number games, word games, and others, which included chess and draughts. Another group had been asked by the teacher to think of other ways of dividing the toys into sets, while the two remaining children had been sent to the school library, with the class helper, to find books about toys of different kinds and about toy-making, list their titles and display them. This involved them in making attractive posters which would draw the attention of the class to the book collection.

By late afternoon, most of the tasks had been satisfactorily completed and the children were able to sort themselves into groups and choose one toy or game to play with, the choices being made in a disciplined way, on the whole, with the teacher as final arbiter.

As, over the weeks, the numbers of toys increased, new categories were defined, so that sorting could be by age – those toys older than the class (some even older than the teacher!) and new toys. Sorting by function was tried and found to be a useful method: water toys, toys for babies, toys for sleeping with, toys for building things, toys which moved, toys to move with (e.g. hoops, skipping ropes, balls, bicycles) and musical toys, were the main categories decided on. Dolls proved difficult because although the collection included male, female and baby dolls, some moved, some made sounds, some were designed for babies, and so on. It was agreed dolls should form a special set which would be divided into sub-groups. Transport toys posed a similar problem; some moved, some did not. Graphs were made showing the numbers of toys which fell into the different categories, and the different ways in which the toys could be sorted.

During this time the teacher read a variety of stories about toys – *Pinocchio* proved a favourite – and the children grew interested in the idea of making puppets. *The Toy Symphony* was used as a basis for their music and movement, and later, when they were spending some time looking at animal toys, *The Carnival of the Animals* was used in a similar way. The work on animal toys led to comparisons with real animals and a world map was used to plot the countries of origin of the various animals.

A visit was arranged to a nearby toy museum, where the children were particularly interested in the old dolls and dolls' houses, puppets and puppet theatres, and lead soldiers. On their return they opted to make puppets and a puppet theatre. It was decided to make stick and glove puppets, because string puppets were likely to be too difficult. This part of the project took up the rest of the half-term. The music to the *The Nutcracker* and *Coppelia* stimulated the children's interest in ballet and a visit to either a puppet theatre or a ballet performance was discussed by the class for the following half-term. A majority preferred the ballet visit because, they said, they were making their own puppets and would be performing their own plays, and while two or three of the girls attended ballet classes, most of the children had never seen a live ballet performance.

At the half-term holiday, since the classroom had become *very* overcrowded, most of the toys were sent home with thanks, except for the dolls, puppets and games, because these were the areas

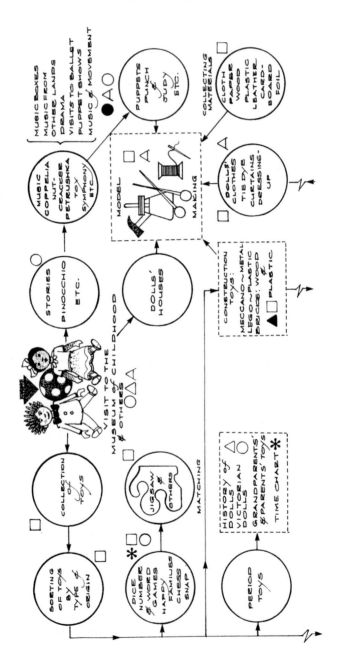

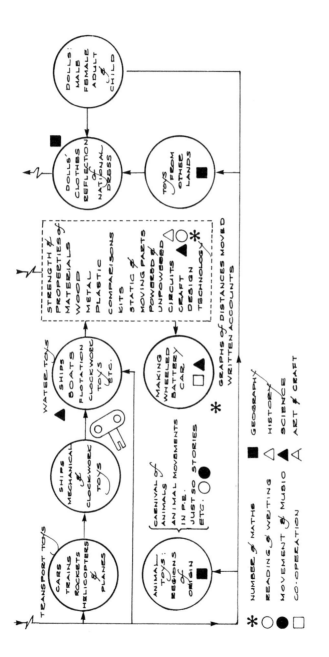

The Toy Project – based on teacher's flow diagram for term's work.

which were going to be further investigated in the following half-term.

The children returned to school still very keen to continue their project and proceeded to divide the dolls into new groups. They decided on dolls for babies, dolls for children (including baby dolls), male and female adult replica dolls, and dolls for ornaments, such as the foreign dressed dolls. Dolls were weighed, and their weights were matched to the materials of their construction. A Victorian peg doll was brought in and an old rag doll was lent. A collector of antique dolls brought in some examples of her collection and the children were overwhelmed to discover the values of some of these.

At the same time they were practising a puppet play to be shown to other classes, and finally to their parents. They were also making up games for themselves, and constructing them out of materials in the classroom, painting them and making up rules. Some of these games were designed to remain in the classroom to be used by the class; others were made as presents for brothers and sisters. As Christmas was approaching, a number of children wanted to make soft toys or carved wooden toys for presents, and a parent who was a wood carver came in to help with this work. The puppet performances took place at the end of the term, and were much appreciated. The visit to the ballet, *The Nutcracker*, could not be fitted in until the beginning of the following term, but was thoroughly enjoyed then.

The teacher evaluated the project with the children by asking them what they thought they had learned. The general view was that they had learned 'a lot'. Some felt they had learned to read better through such things as reading the instructions for games which 'were really hard sometimes'; others had done better writing because it had been for posters and notices to go up in the classroom. Some had learned to play a previously unknown game. Everyone had made something: a puppet or a toy, a woodcarving or a game; some had made several things, and all had done something towards the making of the puppet theatre. Every child had taken part in at least one puppet play, writing his or her own script within their performing group (the scripts could be read rather than learned by heart because only the puppets would be visible to the audience). They all agreed they had learned a lot about toys, how they were made and how much they cost. They had made a book about their toys and their prices. They had learned a lot about making graphs, and, as one said, 'just about how if things don't sort out properly, there's always another way of arranging them'. The teacher said she felt that they had learned to be more considerate with other children's things. They had been introduced to stories and music which they might not otherwise have heard, and they had enjoyed a ballet. Altogether a successful project!

On the canal

This project was begun by adults. A governor of the school, who was also a past parent, had become involved in a campaign to revitalise the local stretch of the Regent's Canal in north London. The canal, little used for many years, had been fenced off, and the area around had become waste ground and a rubbish depository. During the early 1970s the local council started to think of building over it. There had been tragic accidents: children were drawn to the canal, and when children fell in, the fencing prevented adult rescuers reaching them. There was considerable feeling that there was a serious danger which should be got rid of as quickly as possible.

But there were other groups who used the canal. There was a boat club, and they protested that here was a facility for the community, especially for young people, which needed cleaning up and improving. The campaign was joined by others who pointed out that if the fences were taken down and decent play facilities provided on the banks, the children would be in less danger, especially if there were more people around. Gradually the campaign mounted, petitions were signed, schools along the canal took part, and there was a new look at the possibilities. Finally it was decided to fill in only a fraction of the basin and to improve the canalside facilities. Trees were planted, benches were installed, and play areas built. It became a favourite place for studying wild life and many schools began to use it. Our school was a little distance from the canal, but it was close enough to walk to and offered us study facilities which were unique. After discussions between one teacher of top juniors and our enthusiast, plans were made for the following term which included a trip along the canal in a narrow boat.

The interest in the project spread through the school, and other classes began to want to take part, including some infants. All of the classes managed a short trip on the narrow boat; a school on

The Canal Project – based on teacher's flow diagrams.

MAPS

- SOIL & ECOLOGY - - - - - TRANSPORT -
- HABITATION, SETTLEMENTS - FARMING & INDUSTRY
- HYDROLOGICAL CYCLE - - - SEASONS & WEATHER -
- BRIDGES · AQUEDUCTS - - - - TUNNELS & LEGGING'
- 'TURN-OVER' BRIDGES - - - CANAL ARCHITECTURE
VISIT TO MUSEUM AT ⌐ ⌐ ARTWORK & MATHS - -
STOKE BRUERNE ⌋ ⌞ MEASURE - - - - - - -

VISIT TO CIVIL ENGINEER'S OFFICE

⌐ POETRY - - - - - - - - - - - DRAMA - - - - - - - - - -
- SOCIAL STATUS ⌞ SONG & STORY
⌐ COMPARISON WITH ⌐ WORKING BOATS &
⌞ OTHER BOATS ⌋ ⌞ LEISURE BOATS

- WHO PAID?
- MODERN IMMIGRATION
- ROUTES - - - - - - - - - - POEMS, SONGS & DRAMA

⌐ WHAT WAS IT LIKE BEING ⌐ FACTUAL & CREATIVE
A 'NAVVY'? ⌞ WRITING
⌞ SOCIAL STUDIES - - - - - ECONOMICS
- - SAIL & STEAM POWER - - - MODERN POWER
- - EFFECT OF RAIL ⌐ DECLINE & DISUSE - - -
TRANSPORT ⌋ POLLUTION. - - - - - - -
LIVING ON BOARD ~ WHY?

⌐ LOCAL BOAT CLUB
⌐ RECLAMATION ⌞ BOATING
⌞ CANOEING
⌐ FISHING ⌞ WATER SPORTS
⌞ LEISURE PURSUITS - ⌐ WATER SAFETY
- ⌞ WILDLIFE ⌞ TRAINING.
⌐ CONSERVATION
⌞ NATURE WALKS

the canal offered us the use of one of their classrooms so that we could have a local base. The headteacher also kindly lent us canal ware which she had collected during their own canal project. All kinds of work began to develop in the school. One infant class became very interested in canal horses, visited Whitbread's stables, and pursued that line of investigation – and horses, like other animals, are very useful for working out how many legs two, three, four, or five will have between them! More effective than learning tables by rote, but the arithmetic is just the same. Another class of older juniors began to study bridges, and made models, including a working model of a lift bridge, and a model of the lock gates. One of the younger classes discovered toads at the canal and made a study of these.

A longer canal trip was organised for the older classes. Since only about ten children and three adults could be accommodated, groups had to take turns, three days at a time. This was an exercise in planning and self-catering: they had to live together in a confined space, share the navigation of the boat and the opening and closing of the locks. Part of the trip was a visit to the canal museum at Stoke Bruerne in the Midlands. The most adventurous infants also had an overnight trip which they naturally found very exciting.

The older children were very interested in the work of the navvies, and in the contemporary accounts of a terrible explosion in 1874. Some of them empathised greatly with their hardship and wrote poems and imaginary accounts about them:

The people who built the canals were called navvies. The name navvy comes from the word navigator. Navvies had a hard life. A navvy's job is to dig or cut the channel. Navvies didn't make very much and some of their wages were paid in tokens which could only be used in Tommy shops which the company owned. They were exchanged for the goods in the shops. Navvies were killed in every mile, when they built the tunnels.

The tunnels are deep
The tunnels are wide
But we dig and shovel
Just to survive.
We are the navvy men.

We push barrows
Through earth and clay
We work non-stop
Both night and day.
We are the navvy men.

When our work is done
And we reach the tunnel's end
The work begins for the watermen
We are the navvy men.

I was working on the canal as a navvyman, shovelling muck and puddling clay. We fill in holes in the sides of the canal with crushed-up stones. So that we don't get the canals wrong we measure and see that the depth of the canal is right. When we can't go around the hills, we dig through them. We get very little pay for our hard work. We lost sixteen men and we were not allowed to stop and pray for them. We built the locks, the tunnels and we built the waterworks.

It's early morning
My head hurts
My eyes are sore
Grab the pick
Start digging once more

Dig-dig-dig

Sweat running down my head
Back bone breaking
Just to earn my bread
All day long bending,
Pushing, sweating.

Dig-dig-dig

And what's the betting
That I'll never see
This water flow
High and low
Let's finish the job

Dig-dig-dig.

Some of the children visited a narrow boat on which a family lived. Other children interviewed a pensioner who remembered the canal when it had been a busy waterway, in her girlhood. The father of one of the children had actually lived beside the canal when he was a child, and he came and revived his memories for them. A trip was organised, jointly with another school, on a larger boat which took the children through the canal and onto the River Thames, so that they could experience for themselves the link and understand the importance which the canals had before the growth of motor transport.

One class had the idea of a dramatic presentation using the words which the children themselves had written. Some of the poems were put to music, and the narrow boat themes of castles and roses figured largely in the set design. Children throughout the school took part in the final production, the older ones as actors, younger children playing the musical instruments and singing their own song about canal horses. The two performances of *Castles and Roses* were packed and were a fitting culmination for all the varied work which they had done.

Canal views

Although this had all taken more than a year, there were other developments from this project which were to affect the life and work of the school still further. Because the class which had first become involved in the canal work had been a vertically-grouped class, the younger part of the class had still their last year in primary school before them, and they wanted to continue work on some of the themes which had developed from their canal study. One such theme was that of 'reflections' which had been noticed in the water and which became the subject of further investigations of a scientific and mathematical nature as well as prompting discussion on the area of intellectual reflection. These investigations were translated into painting, claywork and poetry:

> The canal is greeny-blue and grey,
> With shiny, rippling reflections
> Of plants growing on disused factory walls.
> Boats on the water,
> Cars in the car-park
> And birds flying up and appearing
> On the surface of the water.

The water is dotted with leaves,
Frothy waves, glossy, dirty pools.
I feel like gliding on the mirror-like water.
Soft shapes on the hard canal edge,
Canal water cascades over the weir.
White, foamy with rage.

A new interest from the canal work had been canoeing, which became part of the regular school physical education curriculum, through the courtesy of the local boat club. This encouraged the children to improve their swimming, in order to qualify for the canoeing course, and they were able to improve their knowledge of water safety procedures.

While not every class in the school covered the same ground, every class had opportunities to extend the project work into several areas of the curriculum. Some classes began with a study of natural history, others with the history or mechanics of the canal. The whole school learned about the local environment and everyone had direct experience of the canal itself; some stayed on a narrow boat and learned about navigation. One infant class produced a book on water safety after their first visit to the canal. There was a great deal of mathematics involved in the model making, including precise measuring and working to scale. There was a lot of vivid writing, a variety of painting and claywork, music and drama. The children learned about archival materials and copied contemporary prints, read and took notes from copies of newspapers from 1874. Finally, they saw their work displayed publicly in the local library and in a teachers' centre, together with the work of other schools which had also been involved in a canal project.

One of the discoveries made by the children during the canal project was that ordinary people like themselves and their families could improve their environment. The campaign which had saved the canals and seen their rebirth as a leisure and educational resource in the area had been organised and fought by local people. This is an important lesson for young people to learn, for they are the citizens of tomorrow and their democratic participation in the running of their community in the future will be vitally important. Their understanding of this need, and their ability to participate, can be strengthened by their being involved in the organisation of their own learning.

As can be seen from this description, an important facility allowed by the project method is that while it gives a clearly-understood structure for both investigation and the improvement of skills, it also provides the flexibility to follow up particular interests which may develop during the course of the project. Thus it allows for spontaneity but prevents that lack of form which characterises some exploratory work and can lead to sloppiness in a primary classroom.

Coda! Getting it right for engineering

While there are never grounds for complacency about education, it is nevertheless just that praise as well as criticism should be noted. At a meeting of the British Association for the Advancement of Science in September 1986, one speaker – Graham Anthony, Industrial Director of the Engineering Council – praised primary teachers for meeting the challenge of science and technology in the classroom. His contribution was reported in *The Teacher* as follows:

> 'Many of the things the Council wants to see done are already at the heart of good primary school practice'. Drawing particular attention to topic work, pupil-centred projects, open-ended learning and across-the-curriculum approaches, he said: 'This is what engineering is about. It is pulling ideas from different parts of the curriculum and different disciplines then putting them together to get an answer'.

Department of Education and Science: please note.

12 | The hidden curriculum

The curriculum is the total experience of school for the child. Thus the learning that takes place, the kind of teaching, the discipline and ethos of the school, all these are part of the school curriculum. In what way then is there a 'hidden' curriculum?

When we do or say something, we expect certain responses from those to whom our words or deeds are directed: we anticipate the outcomes of our speech and actions. But as well as expected outcomes there may be unexpected ones which have arisen for one of a number of reasons. Perhaps our words or deeds have been misunderstood by the recipient, or perhaps our *intentions* have been misunderstood – someone has taken something the wrong way – or, perhaps because we were dissembling in some way, our body language has communicated a message we wanted to keep secret.

In their dealings with children adults often do not say what they mean, and children may be very quick to sense this, for they read our faces as closely as they hear our words. It can be a very destructive thing to think negative thoughts about a child in the child's presence, because they are often sensed and this is painful and damaging to the child's confidence. Some parents and even some teachers (who really should know better) talk to another adult about a child, often critically, in the presence of the subject, but as if he or she were not present. This is something I have always tried to steer people away from; my sympathies have always been with the child, however heinous the crimes committed. Children are young people; they are not some different breed, and as young people they should be treated with the same respect as older people. Because they are learners, because they are young and have different needs and less experience than ourselves, we are in the position of guides. But guidance is not dominance.

How, then, can a school indicate its respect for its pupils? First, by ensuring that the school is a friendly and comfortable place for them, and that from their first visit they are assured of kindness and support there. The environment should be interesting to them and there should be activities on offer which they feel keen to try for themselves. The personnel of a school should speak to the children in a sensible, sympathetic and non-hectoring way. Corporal punishment and shouting at children have no positive function in education.

Unfortunately, because our society is such that many of us, both children and adults alike, are often under considerable strain, we fall short of the ideal. Children know when they have misbehaved and will usually expect to be told so and accept appropriate punishment, so long as they feel that it is fair. On the whole they will model their behaviour on that of the adults around them – perhaps that is what we find so upsetting when they act in a way of which we disapprove; we recognise something of our own behaviour in theirs!

Voices from the past: corporal punishment

> I am altogether opposed to it, first because it is disgusting . . . in the next place, because a pupil . . . will remain obdurate even in the face of blows . . . and finally because such chastisement will be quite unnecessary if there is ever someone present to supervise the boy's studies with diligence . . . If you coerce the young child by means of blows, how would you deal with the grown youth who cannot thus be driven by fear and has more important things to learn?

These words from Quintilian, nearly 2,000 years ago, indicate that opposition to corporal punishment is no soft modern aberration. Others have spoken in the same vein: John Locke, the 17th century philosopher – who was also an opponent of rote learning – wrote:

> The usual lazy and short way, by chastisement, and the rod, which is the only instrument of government that tutors generally know, or ever think of, is the most unfit of any to be used in education . . . beating them, and all sorts of slavish and corporal punishments are not the discipline fit to be used in the education

of those we would have wise, good and ingenuous men; and therefore very rarely to be applied and that only in great occasions and cases of extremity.

As children should very seldom be corrected by blows, so I think frequent and especially, passionate chiding of almost as ill consequence. It lessens the authority of the parents and the respect of the child. A look or a nod ought to correct them when they do amiss. Or if words are sometimes to be used they ought to be grave, kind and sober, representing the ill or unbecomingness of the fault, rather than a hasty rating of the child for it, which makes him not sufficiently distinguish whether your dislike be not more directed to him than his fault.

Although this advice is addressed to parents, it is relevant also for teachers and all who work with children, as is the following wisdom, also from Locke:

He that will have his son have a respect for him and his orders, must himself have a great reverence for his son.

If we make allowance for 17th century sexism, and substitute 'child' for 'son' this statement is as true today as it was then. Nor does this attitude allow for indulgence, which is usually as much self-indulgence for the adult as indulgence for the child.

Comenius opposed corporal punishment:

Beatings are of no use in inculcating a love of school work but they are extremely likely to arouse aversion and hatred for it.

Teaching by example was more positive:

One learns to be virtuous by accomplishing acts of virtue . . . provided always there is someone to show the way by precept and example.

From Hezekiah Woodward's book *Of the Child's Portion*, comes the following advice to parents:

It is their charge whereof they must give an exact account –

yea, of every part and parcel of this seed-time . . . The conduct and bearing of the parents is the child's book from which he learns to speak and hear.

What we teach without meaning to

While it is undoubtedly true that parents have this major influence over their children, it is also true that teachers are very influential as well: schools can make a difference. The school in which a child is treated with respect will encourage the child to have respect for others. The school in which a child is listened to will help the child to listen to others. It is fairly common knowledge that in a classroom where the teacher has a loud voice, the children will speak more loudly, whereas if a teacher speaks very quietly, the children will be likely to do so too. Once, while teaching an infant class, I heard a six-year-old girl say to another child, in a voice dripping with sarcasm, 'Oh, very clever!' I recognised my own voice in hers; if a child did something foolish, thoughtless, and there was an untoward result, I would say something sarcastic! It shocked me and taught me to think more carefully about what I said in the classroom.

Clearly, the way teachers speak to their children, their manner towards them, as well as the content of their speech, are all influential. If we want the children whom we teach to be thoughtful, we must be thoughtful towards them; it is we who set the example. If we want children to think for themselves, we must encourage this by listening to their ideas and treating them with respect. If we genuinely think we always know best, we probably should not be teaching anyway. A school is a partnership of teachers, children, other school staff and parents. So the way their parents are treated is also a key question for the children. Are their parents respected and welcomed in the school? If they are not, what are we communicating to the children about the way we view them and their families? The way teachers treat each other and their attitude to the non-teaching staff of the school are all factors influencing the way children will regard the adults around them.

If we want children to value school property and treat it with respect, and respect the work and property of other children, then we must treat their work and property with respect. Children very often lose articles of clothing at school; they get very anxious about this, and their anxieties need to be treated seriously and real attempts made to find the missing articles, even if they have been lost through the child's own carelessness. This might seem very trivial, but it is not trivial to the children, nor to the parents. Such a situation can be a learning point for the child, but not if it turns into resentment because then the child feels that no adult made the effort to help, even if that feeling is unwarranted. It is important for the child to feel supported in such situations. It is also important for parents to minimise such disasters by ensuring that their children's clothing is always clearly named; it is small things such as this which can prevent distress to the child and time-wasting searches for the teacher.

There are many things which might worry a small child, which seem minor to adults. It is never enough to say 'Never mind' and forget all about it. Small worries grow into great nightmares and parents should talk seriously to a child who is worried, and if necessary, raise the matter with the teacher or headteacher. Teachers also find that spending five minutes sorting out a minor problem can save hours of long-winded investigation of a more serious matter at a later date.

Above all, children need to know their teachers are on *their* side, that they do their best to keep them out of trouble of all kinds. There are some teachers who seem to delight in issuing threats, reporting children to the headteacher, and giving punishments. This has a deeply negative effect on children and obstructs their ability to learn with that teacher. That is not to say that wrong-doing should go unpunished – the teacher is responsible for protecting the other children from disturbance or harassment – but rather that the teacher's concern should be prevention rather than punishment. Discussion with the child, to find out the motive for anti-social acts, and conveying to the child that, while the teacher dislikes the action, he or she has never stopped liking the child, will pay far more dividends than threats could ever do. Teachers should never be punitive, or in the child's eyes they may become an enemy – which is not a relationship conducive to learning, and that, after all, is what children come to school for; that is why the school exists.

Food for thought

School dinners are a kind of joke issue; it is fashionable among children to complain about them. And in the past there has certainly been a lot of foolishness on the part of adults involved with their production. Now that they are being threatened and have even been removed in some local authority areas, their role seems all the more important. Many school dieticians have been very slow indeed to respond to what the medical profession has been stating for some time: that there was too much sugar and animal fat in our diets, and that this is especially bad for children. What opportunities have been missed for educating generations of future parents about food values! Instead there has been the constant excuse: 'We have to give the children what they like or they won't eat it.' This is not true; I have seen thousands of children introduced to fresh vegetables who, if the food was well cooked and not overcooked, ate them with gusto. Very many quite young children like vegetarian food, where this is provided and prepared imaginatively. In the cities now, where the school population is ethnically mixed, there is a wide range of dishes which can be offered to children and which they enjoy.

When the school in which I was headteacher had regular International Food Evenings, in which parents brought in dishes from all parts of the globe, I would stand and watch the children tucking in to curries, kebabs, salads and humus. Dishes from Ireland, Africa, India, Turkey, Greece, Wales, Scotland, Italy, and Hong Kong would disappear as readily as native dishes like sausage rolls or shepherd's pie. The food which children learn to eat at school is also part of the curriculum we offer them, and like everything else, it should be of high quality. When we value and enjoy the food of other ethnic groups, we also show our respect for them, a lesson children are not slow to understand, and this is a useful tool in increasing anti-racist awareness. There is enough junk food for both mind and body available outside school. The job of the school is to give the children a standard by which they can measure what is on offer, and reject that which is not worth having or which is harmful.

The real message

So the hidden curriculum comes more clearly into view; all the experiences of the child, both inside and outside the classroom, contribute to it. Are the school lavatories ones you, as an adult, would be prepared to use? If they are not, then they are not fit for the children to use either. If we allow them to use unappealing lavatories, what are we telling them about our opinion of them? If the school playground is bleak and unattractive, what does that tell them? If their school day is hedged about with rules for which they can see no reason, what does that tell them about our expectations of them? If we never ask their opinion about their school activities and arrangements, how can we expect them to be fully involved in them? It is important to know how children regard their school, and we can learn from their opinions.

School councils are one way of involving children, at least from the age of seven. Some younger children might even be able and willing to participate. Another way is to have some of the older children attending governors' meetings as pupil observers for non-confidential items, and reporting back to the other children in the school and answering their questions. This can also be of practical value:

> At the time the nursery block was being built, the pupil observers played a key role in conveying information about the proposed changes to the rest of the school. Everyone was deeply interested in the progress of the work and many looked forward to seeing their own young brothers and sisters in the new class. At a governors' meeting at which the plans for fencing off an area of the playground for the use of the nursery children were being discussed, one pupil observer, who was eyeing the plans keenly, asked if he could speak. He pointed out that the fencing on the side adjacent to the main playground (used for ball games) ought to be much higher than that of the other sides of the playground, to stop balls flying over and hitting the small children. This had not occurred to the architect nor to the other adults examining the plans. His suggestion was welcomed and incorporated into the plans and he was able to report this back proudly the next day. (*Pupil Observers at one London Primary School*, Forum, 1984)

Children see things from their own viewpoint, and this is often different from that of an adult, but it is nevertheless always worth listening to: we might well learn something of value. Certainly the hidden curriculum conveys to children whether or not it is worth their while having ideas of their own and how their ideas will be received if they are expressed.

In the same way, when children are in streamed classes, they all know their place in the hierarchy – no-one needs to tell them formally, they absorb the information as if by osmosis, but actually from the attitudes they perceive and indirectly from what is said both to them and in their hearing. Children become aware of the expectations of teachers and parents even when these are not overtly expressed. That is why our hidden beliefs and prejudices are even more damaging than those which have surfaced.

The school's policy on equal opportunities will also be felt by pupils. If it doesn't exist, then the school will exert a negative influence. If we convey to girls that we don't expect them to be able to make progress in scientific work, or play football, or convey to boys that we don't expect them to show emotion, or take care of smaller children, they will respond by trying to conform to our prejudices – unless they are rebellious, in which case they may become objects of our displeasure, difficult, unco-operative or a nuisance. Even more damaging, of course, is the teacher who unwittingly equates educability with a middle-class background, or skin colour, and thereby undermines children who are working class or black.

Competition or co-operation

There have been recent media criticisms of schools where, it is said, competitive sports are no longer allowed because of 'progressive' ideas. This is another example of the 'either-or' outlook, which insists that different things have to be mutually exclusive. A co-operative ethos does not have to exclude all competition, but it can encourage competition against one's own previous best efforts as well as against the efforts of others. There is no reason why excellence cannot be worked for and applauded because children work together. There is a place for both, so long as it is understood that, in social terms, more can be achieved through co-operation, while different things can be won in competition – things which lead to a sense of individual achievement. It is also true that most individual personal triumphs in competitive situations, such as sport, also rest on previous training which involves a team, and therefore co-operation. Competitive sport also involves co-operation in team games. What anyone in schools must oppose is the kind of competitiveness that thinks winning is the *only* object in playing, which can lead to the kind of outlook in which it is legitimate to cheat and lie in order to win. We all have to learn to lose as well as win, and we ought to be able to admire superior skills when we meet them even though they are shown by an opponent.

In fact the achievement of excellence in any area, whether in sport, music or mathematics, depends not so much on competitiveness as on widespread opportunities for children to develop whatever potential they have. An emphasis on competition often results in those showing the most promise being selected for special treatment far too early. This kind of elitism narrows the base from which potentially excellent performances can be drawn. This is because our selection procedures are not infallible and because children do not develop at regular rates. It was precisely this which was wrong with our old 11-plus selection procedure: large numbers of bright children were kept out of grammar school, which was a great waste of talent. If more resources were made available to wider sections of people in this country, then more talent would emerge. If we want the pyramid to reach higher in the heavens, we must enlarge the base. Elitism is self-defeating, and where it is present in the hidden curriculum it serves to narrow opportunity and depress standards.

Knowing what we mean and meaning what we say

The way in which schools are organised and run; the attitudes of teachers and other staff towards children and their parents: these are the hidden curriculum. Children soon respond to our expectations of them. This hidden curriculum is highly influential and it can be decisive in convincing children that it is worth their while to make real efforts in learning, because everyone in the school has confidence in their ability to learn and is prepared to help them in this endeavour. This can be a strength even to those children who, for whatever reason, are not assisted in this way at home.

The hidden curriculum needs to support and strengthen the stated curriculum. In some schools, it works against it. If we have a school policy which announces that all children should have equal opportunities, but go on asking for some 'strong boys' to help carry something, or always rely on 'sensible girls' to clear up, then our hidden curriculum will be undermining our stated aims. If we have an anti-racist policy but still accept stereotyped images such as 'black children all have rhythm' or 'Asian children are well-behaved', or indicate by our manner, or our refusal to make a real effort to understand what is being said to us, that those who do not speak standard English are inferior to ourselves, or less intelligent in some way, then we are defeating our own policy. If a school is so determinedly 'high culture' that working-class children and parents feel alien, then we are contributing to deprivation. Contradictions between stated policies and their applications can cause tensions which are detrimental to learning. Schools *can* make a difference to children's lives, so we must know what is really being taught.

13 | Private progressive schools

When people think about 'progressive' education, they often have a picture in their minds of the schools which they have read about in the press, schools like Dartington or Summerhill, which have for many years been part of the independent progressive school movement. These schools, which cater for children of both primary and secondary age, had their origins in a parental revolt.

The last decade of the 19th century saw the foundation of many schools which claimed to be adherents of the 'new' or 'progressive' education. They were essentially products of discontent with the public school system, which was hierarchical and had institutionalised corporal punishment. Intellectual, liberal, middle-class parents wanted more gentle, civilised, schools for their young. Bertrand Russell, in his book *On Education*, wrote about Arnold of Rugby:

> Dr Arnold was the great reformer of our public schools, which are viewed as one of the glories of England, and are still conducted largely according to his principles. In discussing Dr Arnold, therefore, we are dealing, not with something belonging to the remote past, but with something which to this day is efficacious in moulding upper-class Englishmen. Dr Arnold diminished flogging, retaining it only for the younger boys, and confining it, so his biographer tells us, to 'moral offences, such as lying, drinking and habitual idleness'. But when a liberal journalist suggested that flogging was a degrading punishment, which ought to be abolished altogether, he was amazingly indignant.

And later in the book:

> Dr Arnold's system, which has remained in force in English

153

public schools to the present day, had another defect, namely that it was aristocratic. The aim was to train men for positions of authority and power, whether at home or in distant parts of the empire. An aristocracy, if it is to survive, needs certain virtues; these were imparted at school. The product was to be energetic, stoical, physically fit, possessed of certain unalterable beliefs, with high standards of rectitude, and convinced that it had an important mission in the world. To a surprising extent, these results were achieved. Intellect was sacrificed to them. because intellect might produce doubt. Sympathy was sacrificed, because it might interfere with governing 'inferior' races or classes. Kindliness was sacrificed for the sake of toughness, imagination for the sake of firmness.

New schools were sought which would be more humane. The Parents' National Education Union, formed in 1887, opened a training college in the theory and methods of education at Ambleside, in 1892. A growing number of parents were ready to support the new schools.

The first of these was Abbotsholme, established by Cecil Reddie in 1889, which contained elements of progressive education in that it included a great deal of practical work in its curriculum:

> Boys were to learn the rudiments of agriculture and gardening and the care of animals, which besides anything else would be a sound preparation for colonial life.

> Abbotsholme was intended as a school for boys belonging to the directing classes and while it was enlightened in many respects such as uniform and the teaching of hygiene, including sex instruction, all aspects of school life were dominated by Reddie himself. (*The Educational Innovators*, W.A.C. Stewart)

Bedales was founded by J.H. Badley, an Abbotsholme master, in 1893; it was less orthodox and doctrinaire, more democratic and later became co-educational. The King Alfred School Society was founded in 1897 and among the objects for which it was established was:

> To give practical expression to the best theories of education extant, and particularly to the theories enunciated by educational

reformers such as Pestalozzi, Froebel, Herbart, Herbert Spencer, Louis Compton Miall, and others working on similar lines.

Of all the schools founded at this time, the King Alfred School was the one most firmly and consciously based on the principles of progressive education, and it is still flourishing in Hampstead.

The years after the First World War saw a rapid growth in the number of independent progressive schools – Tiptree Hall, Rendcomb College, Summerhill, Dartington, Beacon Hill, among them. Some of these were experimental and their emphasis was very much on 'atmosphere' and 'freedom to grow' rather than on curriculum. There was a great deal of innovation, but little monitoring to see how well it was working, at least at first.

Some of the schools appear to have been concerned primarily with the establishment of a democratic society within which children possessed a considerable degree of autonomy and were largely self-directed, rather than with curriculum. The most important considerations were those of morality rather than intellect, and children were not compelled to attend classes. The most extreme example was Summerhill, established in the 1920s by A.S. Neill, a man with a great love of children, but a great lack of interest in curriculum. He wrote in *That Dreadful School*:

> Personally I do not know what kind of teaching is carried on for I never visit lessons and have no interest in how children learn. We have no new methods of teaching because we do not consider that teaching very much matters.

Nor was he alone in holding this point of view. W.B. Currie of Dartington echoed it in his book, *Dartington Hall*:

> I have never been able to get excited over teaching methods and I have felt that most gifted teachers, at any rate, arrive at their own methods. Nor have I ever been able to get excited over curriculum.

That headteachers responsible for the education of numerous children should make such statements seems incredible today. But in the period between the wars, it seems to have been an acceptable point of view! In later years, when HMI were to inspect Summerhill in 1949, they reported that, while there was a great degree of freedom:

> On the whole the results of this system are unimpressive. It is true that children work with a will and an interest that is most refreshing, but their achievements are rather meagre. This is not, in the inspectors' opinion, an inevitable result of the system, but of the system working badly. . . Some surprisingly old-fashioned and formal methods are in use.

A surprising situation: HMI, far from attacking Summerhill for being too progressive, criticised the school for being too formal and old-fashioned in its teaching! Instead of a progressive curriculum being developed, Neill's lack of interest in this area, surely the key area in any school, had adversely affected its development.

On the other hand, J.H. Badley, the founder of Bedales, in his autobiographical account of that school, puts emphasis on a 'balanced, broad curriculum', in the earlier stages of which the object is to:

> Awaken interests and bring the child into contact with many kinds of experience in order to give a wide basis of the simpler kinds of knowledge and a keen enjoyment of the use of his powers; and in the latter stages, it must rather be directed to intensifying interest in certain directions and to practising certain kinds of intellectual discipline as the means of gaining whatever special knowledge may be required. (*Bedales*, J.H. Badley)

Unlike Neill, Badley taught classes himself and was involved in both curriculum development and evaluating its results, so that curriculum change took place there over the years. The Bedales prospectus indicated a more authoritarian structure there too:

> The first lesson a child must learn is absolute obedience to authority . . . We obviously cannot let a child do only or entirely what he likes; too much time may be lost and certain necessary lessons remain unlearned, and if each goes his own way he will inevitably get into someone else's.

There were clearly many differences among different progressive schools. Some were more authoritarian, and even retained caning; the Quaker schools were far more open to absence of restraint, and a teacher working there at that time was quoted as saying:

> We find no imposed control and no self-control. I do not want the former, but I do seek after the latter. . . Every community is built on a slave class. Here it is the staff. (*Quakers and Education*, W.A.C. Stewart)

Unless the schools were very well-endowed (as were the Quaker schools), they did have one thing in common: they were all fee-paying. Whatever the personal convictions of their founders, and although some might from time to time have taken a 'deserving' case free or for a low fee, the schools had to pay their way. It is interesting to note that in a 1961 survey, 81 per cent of parents of private progressive school pupils belonged to social classes I and II. None at all came from group V.

Facts such as these, and the identification of 'progressive education' with these schools, has contributed to a mistaken notion that progressive education is some kind of middle-class phenomenon, associated with permissiveness, rather than an expression of the developmental tradition in education. A school should be judged on its classrooms, as well as on its stated objectives, or its ethos – in any case the ethos of the school should permeate its classrooms and is also transmitted through its curriculum. When a school is a boarding school, and most of the independent progressive schools are, it has to provide a home as well as an education for its pupils. The reaction against the harshness of the conventional public schools might have led to more emphasis on the former than the latter, but there appears to have been a mismatch in many of these schools between what went on inside and outside the classrooms. And they were certainly not known for their development of a progressive curriculum which would advance children's learning.

Whether they were truly progressive or not, there has been a general media bias against such schools because of what is seen as their progressive nature. In his *Considering Children*, David Gribble, who was a teacher at Dartington for many years, but had himself attended Eton, wrote about the anti-progressive bias of the press which effectually pilloried Dartington and its headmaster. He pointed out that in 1983 there were press reports of boys expelled and suspended from Eton for vandalising a village church, others reported expelled from Stowe for drug usage, more similarly from Repton, and still others from Eton for smoking cannabis, as well as a report of a dead baby found in a locker at Badminton, but none of these occurrences got the kind of front-page treatment that was bestowed on Dartington Hall. Misbehaviour, and even crimes committed, by pupils at the so-called traditional public schools are not seen as the responsibility of those schools, whereas anything done at a so-called progressive school is immediately attributed to the educational system there.

Schools with a difference

When HMI visited the Rudolf Steiner school, Michael Hall, Sussex, in 1930, they reported:

> We have visited many types of school in this country. The ethical colourings in those schools might be different according to whether they were state, public, private, denominational, progressive and the rest, but the actual education offered was essentially the same in all of them. This is the first school we have met in which the philosophy of the school has totally altered the character of the education offered.

In what way were the Rudolf Steiner schools so different? There were three main phases in their education, as L.F. Edmunds explains in *Rudolf Steiner Education*, published in 1962. The first was the nursery, where:

> The fullest scope is given to spontaneity in play, in art, in movement, in drama, in folk and fairy-tales and in seasonal festivals, the archetypes of experience.

Then there was the period from seven to 14, when:

> If the heart forces are not educated rightly, the intellect, left to itself, isolates men one from another . . Then we have parties but not community. The education we are describing sets out to try to overcome the primary evil, egotism.

The third phase was adolescence, when Steiner saw the beginning of independent life of thought, somewhat reminiscent of Piaget's stage of formal operations. But Steiner found 'two antithetical difficulties in adolescence: egotism in material things and scepticism in spiritual things'. The remedy for these problems could be found in art.

Rudolf Steiner began as a theosophist, but moved beyond this into anthroposophy. He opened a school in 1919 for the children of operatives in the Waldorf Astoria cigarette factory in Stuttgart, the Freie Waldorfschule, which became the model for other Steiner schools throughout the world. The first Steiner school in Britain was opened in Streatham in 1925 and later transferred to Sussex, becoming known as Michael Hall. Since then the number of Steiner schools has increased greatly.

For Steiner, true reality was spiritual and not material; in the schools, democracy and choice were not part of the school's aim. Authority was vested in the adults and there was a slower educational pace. Nor was the curriculum shaped by the demands of an examination syllabus. Spiritual development was the main aim and intellectual growth was secondary. The impressive work done with mentally handicapped children in Steiner homes is a manifestation of this belief, for it is only the physical body, the intellect, which is damaged. Beneath this lives the immortal spirit which can be reached through art and music rather than through the intellect.

The kindergarten

Pre-school education has in the past always been privately-financed; although a minority of nursery places are now provided by some of the education authorities, most provision remains in the private sector and is largely a middle-class preserve. In fact nowadays the children of the wealthy, the aristocracy and even royalty become pupils at the most select establishments. The term 'kindergarten', which has become synonymous with pre-school education in some parts of the world, is properly associated with the ideas of Friedrich Froebel, who originated the idea. He had, like Herbart, worked with Pestalozzi. Herbart and Pestalozzi had based their theories on their practical work with children and on their observations, emphasising the importance of nurture rather than nature. Froebel, on the other hand, reasoned deductively and based his prescriptions upon his theoretical construct of the nature of man. He himself had an unhappy childhood, his mother dying during his infancy and he being neglected by his pastor father, who later remarried. Froebel was an unsuccessful scholar, became interested in forestry and agriculture and from this developed an interest in the natural sciences. He became intensely mystical and felt that this was a natural and intrinsic element in boyhood. In a letter to a friend in 1828, he wrote:

> I was very early impressed with the contradictions of life in word and deed . . . Thus in my tenth and eleventh years I came to dream of life as a connected whole without contradictions. Everywhere to find life, harmony, freedom from contradictions and to recognise with a keener and clearer perception the life unity after which I dimly groped.

Throughout his writings he returns to the themes of contradiction and unity: the Trinity was another concept which held deep meaning for him. He was impressed by the inter-connectedness of all things, which he saw as a manifestation of the Trinity of God. Each child was a unique individual and the unity of life was expressed through the child, for the Trinity was also manifest in the family – father, mother and child. Since the child's inner being contained Godness, the child must be good, it could not be otherwise. The role of the educator was not to interfere, but to allow the unimpeded flowering of the child, just as the wise gardener allowed the unimpeded blossoming of his plant. From this comes the word 'kindergarten', or 'garden of children'. He published *The Education of Man* in 1826, a book in which pedagogy, or the science of teaching, is inextricably interwoven with metaphysics. In it he puts forward the following view of education:

> Education in instruction and training originally and in its first principles, should necessarily be passive, following (only guarding and protecting), not prescriptive, categorical, interfering.

and of the school:

> Never forget that the essential business of the school is not so

much to teach and to communicate a variety and multiplicity of things, as it is to give prominence to the ever-living unity that is in all things.

He conceived the idea of a number of 'gifts' which he insisted were more than toys or apparatus; they were symbols of the child's own developing consciousness of the universe. The first gift consisted of a box of six coloured worsted balls (the ball or sphere was a symbol of perfection and represented Froebel's own fundamental symbolic principles in education and life). The next combined a wooden ball with a cylinder and cube; then came the two-inch wooden cube which divided into eight one-inch cubes; then came cuboids, rods, triangles and four-sided prisms – all useful mathematical and spatial apparatus.

The kindergarten used singing and mime games, reminiscent of the way in which Pestalozzi's Gertrude did, as a basis for graduated exercises which were thought to be appropriate to the stage the children had reached. But these were more formal than those which Pestalozzi had promoted. Self-activity and the child's experience were said to be the basis for all education. But whereas Pestalozzi had put great emphasis on the child learning by doing, as had Comenius, Rousseau and Herbart, there are grounds for thinking that in the case of the Froebelian kindergarten the condition was fulfilled if children merely *played* at doing.

While Froebel contributed to the increasing awareness of the importance of play in early childhood, the children attending his kindergarten were, of course, from middle-class families who could pay fees. Whereas Gertrude's children had learned to perform household tasks through her games, the kindergarten children pretended to be doing them. This imparted a certain 'twee-ness' to the kindergarten movement which contrasted sharply with the Montessori schools, although this distinction has been blurred now, at least in this country, where both Froebelian and Montessori schools have become the prerogative of the children of the well-to-do. This is particularly ironic since Maria Montessori intended her nursery schools to be for the children of the poorest Romans.

The Children's Houses

The Montessori method was very much concerned with developing children's competence in the real world. The children spent time handling real objects; they set tables for meals, they moved chairs quietly, used sandpaper letters, looked after animals and plants. They counted on the Montessori 'stair' apparatus, and learned to work together as a group. The Children's Houses gave more preparation for later schooling, something which was anathema to the Froebelians.

Dr Maria Montessori had worked in the psychiatric clinic of Rome University and this had given her a special knowledge of the physiological needs of young children. When she opened the first *Casa dei Bambini* (Children's House) in Rome she described the conditions under which working families and their children were living in the industrial centre of Rome. This situation horrified her for she believed children were profoundly affected by their environment. The improvement of the quality of life for the slum dwellers became a major aim for her. In her own book, *The Montessori Method*, she wrote:

> Scientific pedagogy will seek in vain to better the new generation if it does not succeed in influencing also the environment within which this new generation grows.

The development of a scientific pedagogy was another of her aims. The Children's Houses were areas of experiment and the directors, whose interventions had to be delicately determined, also had the role of observing the children's behaviour. The health of the children was an important factor; they were measured and weighed and given regular medical checks. Mothers were encouraged to visit and take part in bathing their children, and hygiene was taught to mothers and children. Many of the mothers, themselves reared in slums and without sanitation in their homes, would have had no opportunities for health education previously. Diet was carefully considered and only those foods thought to be suitable for young children were served.

She invented various pieces of apparatus to be used by the children, which she believed could compensate for the experiences which were commonly enjoyed by children in the countryside, or by better-off city children with gardens, but which were not open to her children from the slums.

Montessori emphasised the child's interest in the process of doing, rather than in the finished product. She saw that those who did things for children, rather than teaching them to do things for themselves, impede their progress. She stated that children were often treated like puppets, washed and fed as if they were dolls. *We do not stop to think that the child who does not do, does not know how to do.* She argued that those for whom everything must be done, whether through incompetence or status, are equally dependent. Only those who can act for themselves in every area of life could be independent. So the task of education was to help children achieve this independence, and the road to competence was through self-activity.

Montessori wanted the children to have as much liberty as possible, and to have the freedom to make mistakes, but she, like many other progressive educators, put limits upon this: children were not to be free to disturb others. The child who persisted in anti-social behaviour was first investigated by a physician to determine whether or not he or she was normal. If found to be normal, the child was isolated from the other children, placed in a comfortable chair and given favourite games and toys, able to watch the others at their occupations, but not mix with them. The child was treated rather as if ill, and the teacher would approach gently, speak quietly, and ask if he or she felt quite well. Eventually the child expressed a desire to rejoin the others, and usually the lesson was effective, according to Dr Montessori's book. However, it should be added that if the procedure was not effective the Rules and Regulations of the Houses allowed for the expulsion of 'those who show themselves to be incorrigible'!

Children began to learn about discipline very early, for self-discipline, like self-activity was basic to the Montessori method. She felt that it was vital that children learned early to distinguish between good and evil and that formal education seemed to encourage the belief that good was synonymous with immobility and evil with activity, and this was something she wanted to reverse in the minds of her pupils.

Montessori saw that when children were engrossed in what they were doing because it had significance for them, external rewards and punishments had no real effect. The prize was in the doing and in the sense of achievement gained. She remarked that great deeds were rarely carried out for material gain; in fact the opposite often obtained and sometimes martyrdom was the outcome, yet even this did not deter those who were inspired by great ideas.

Domestic developments

By the time Montessori's work became widely known in Britain, the kindergarten was already firmly established on Froebelian principles. The Froebel Society had been founded in 1874 by Maria Grey and others, and many private kindergartens were opened in the years which followed, some employing German teachers. During the early years of the century the Froebelians also opened free kindergartens for slum children in major cities – a new departure. Thus by 1912 when *The Montessori Method* was published the Froebelians were firmly entrenched in Britain and exhibited hostility towards the new ideas. Some educationists resented Montessori's insistence that her whole package must be adopted – she refused to allow for any adaptation of her ideas. Sadly, this doctrinaire attitude became characteristic of the followers of both Froebel and Montessori, although there were many who saw value in both methods and who would like to have developed a new synthesis. It is possible that the cause of progressive education might have been better served had there been fewer schisms among its leading exponents.

Among supporters of Maria Montessori's ideas was Edmond Holmes, former Chief Inspector of Elementary Schools, and a leading supporter of progressive education. In 1911 he wrote a book on the subject called *What Is and What Might Be*. He persuaded other educationists to visit her in Rome and one, Rev Cecil Grant of St George's School in Harpenden, opened a Montessori class adjacent to his senior school on his return, and persuaded Dr Montessori to visit and speak at Harpenden in 1919. Another Montessori supporter was Beatrice Ensor, who was editor of *New Era*, the journal of the New Education Fellowship which in the early decades of this century chronicled progressive schools with examples of curriculum innovation – like the Ellerslie Road School in west London where the children played multiplication tables in the playground using themselves as counters. She wrote: 'In our opinion the Montessori system is a most valuable element in the forward movement in education, and we propose to devote a few pages to this subject every quarter.'

In the early years of the 20th century the nursery school movement had rested almost entirely upon the efforts of Rachel and Margaret McMillan who, like Montessori, were concerned with the children of the poorest sections of the population, with their health and nutrition as well as their education. This led to the opening of 'camp schools' in which boys and girls from the slums lived, worked and slept in the open air as far as possible.

Another school to be based on Montessori principles was the Malting House School in Cambridge. It opened in 1924 with Susan Isaacs in charge, and was run as an experimental children's community with as little adult interference as possible. This school was financed by a businessman, Geoffrey Pyke, but unfortunately after his suffering a financial crash, the school had to be closed in 1929. There was a great deal of attention paid to the children's health and physical well-being, There was plenty of space, fresh air and trees to climb, careful attention was paid to the food, and the Montessori sensory apparatus formed a basis for the children's academic learning.

Susan Isaacs had been influenced by Freud and by John Dewey. She was concerned to educate children so that they would be free from the trauma introduced in previous generations by sexual inhibitions, and to make a study of children's behaviour on which a more scientific pedagogy could be developed. She wrote of the school:

The children are free to explore and experiment with the physical world, the way things are made, the fashion in which they break and burn, the properties of water and gas and electric light, the rain, sunshine, the mud and the frost. They are free to create either by fantasy in imaginative play or by real handling of clay and wood and bricks. The teacher is there to meet this free inquiry and activity by his skill in bringing together the material and the situations which may give children the means of answering their own questions about the world. (*Adventures in Education*, Van der Eyken and Turner)

The detailed observations made by Susan Isaacs, together with case histories of her pupils, formed the basis of her books which were to be instrumental in revolutionising ideas of child development. Her husband, Nathan Isaacs, also wrote booklets introducing the work of Piaget, with whom the Isaacs were in touch. When she later became Head of the Child Development Department at the London Institute of Education, she became a major influence upon large numbers of teaching students.

The effect of the work of these progressive pioneers, both practical and theoretical, has been to emphasise the importance of pre-school education for children's development. Where home conditions are particularly advantageous and adults have ample time to spend with young children, and where the children have access to a wide range of activities and the company of other children, then perhaps nursery school experience is not so important. However, the pre-school playgroup movement has grown up precisely because these favourable home conditions are not so easily provided. Unfortunately, a major part of pre-school provision remains in the private sector because local authorities are unable to finance the classes which are needed to offer nursery education to every child whose parents desire it, although the 1944 Education Act laid down that it should be so provided.

The range of education for all ages available to those able to pay fees has been, and still is, wide. It encompasses both traditions in education, and standards vary tremendously. There are undoubtedly private progressive schools – from nursery to secondary – in existence today which fulfill all the curricular requirements of progressive schooling, except that fee-paying schools, by their very nature, must be elitist. Quite clearly a number of privately-financed schools have contributed to the spread of some progressive ideas, but that contribution has not always been helpful because it has focused the argument on ethos rather than curriculum, and some episodes have linked the term 'progressive education' with 'permissiveness', which is, in no way, embedded in the mainstream of progressive practice.

14 | Design for education

School buildings come in all shapes and sizes, depending upon when they were built. Many have been adapted, with varying degrees of success, in an effort to make them more congenial for modern educational ideas. They are also non-transferable: they remain at their original sites although population shifts and urban development have made those sites inconvenient or (in the case of schools situated on busy main roads) dangerous to children. Yet even if, by some miracle, a government were to decide on a very expensive and radical building programme designed to give each locality the most suitable school buildings on optimum sites, within a few years these would probably have become less suitable and the sites, without very strict building controls, might once again become less desirable than they were. The kind of school buildings we have and their position within local communities are not simple matters, but ones which are subject to many constraints. The architecture of a school will be shaped by the educational ideas of the time and by financial considerations. School positions will be determined by the availability of sites and by demographic predictions. And so it has been the case in the past that the buildings and their sites were determined by the prevailing philosophy, the availability of land, and the search for low costs:

When the problem of mass elementary education was first faced in the early 19th century educationists inevitably took as their model the type of schoolrooms which had been usual in England since the later Middle Ages. The original schoolroom at Winchester, as at Eton and Harrow and other, less famous, schools, consisted simply of one very large room, in various parts of which the forms were taught by a number of assistant masters or 'ushers'. Qualified assistants could not be afforded for the new elementary schools of the early 19th century and monitors were employed to take groups of children under the supervision of a single master or mistress. (*Primary School Design*, Malcolm Seaborne)

This design was then varied by the introduction of a gallery, a stepped floor on which children could sit, and which was used for oral lessons for the younger children. In 1851 the Committee of Council on Education recommended the addition of a classroom for separate lessons, and this model was widely adopted, especially in rural areas. Several classes would be taught in the main schoolroom, with curtains pulled between the sections where pupil teachers would pass on whatever knowledge they themselves had gained, with the aid of the blackboard.

Strangely it was the Revised Code of 1862, discussed in chapter 3, which created a demand for some divisions within the school. Because of the emphasis on 'standards' it involved some degree of subdivision for different age groups. While in America and Europe schools were being designed with completely separate classrooms, because so many of the teachers in England were unqualified pupil teachers, this trend could not be followed. Instead a compromise was worked out, a central hall with small areas leading out of it. This proved a design which seriously impeded curricular change in the years to come.

It was the bigger school boards in major cities which, after the 1870 Education Act, were faced with the problem of building schools for a large and still-growing child population. The London School Board, in particular, was looking for solutions and by and large these were to build larger schools with individual classrooms opening off a corridor, or a central hall with classrooms opening off three or four sides. Many such schools are still in use in urban areas. Later, specialist rooms such as drawing rooms and cookery centres were included in the school buildings.

The curriculum followed by the pupils would then depend very much upon where a child went to school. A girl attending one of the old voluntary schools, built earlier in the century, was unlikely to receive any cookery lessons, while another who was enrolled in one of the newer board schools with a cookery centre installed would have the advantage of such instruction.

Special schools

The introduction of the first 'special schools', for children with a variety of special needs, by the London School Board, also had an effect. Twenty-four such schools were opened between 1892 and 1896. These schools were to have classrooms for not more than 30 children, a great advance at a time when some classes were probably double that size. Seaborne and Lowe write in their book, *The English School: Its Architecture and Organisation*:

> These early 'special schools' were usually built in the playgrounds of large board schools and were single storey with four or five classrooms and 'hall corridors' 15 feet wide. They bore a striking resemblance in layout to some of the first pavilion schools designed more than a decade later by provincial architects. Teaching methods in these schools were almost revolutionary by the standards of the day.

They also quote the headmistress of one such special school, built in the playground of Hugh Myddleton School in London, in 1896:

> The strict discipline so necessary in the large classes of the ordinary school I do not encourage, as I feel the full development of the child is hindered rather than helped by it.

She went on to explain that in her own school:

> He is allowed to ask questions and to hold conversations with his teacher on what he has seen in the hope that his mind will be expanded. The afternoon session, with its varied occupations, is still the most popular in all the classes.

This same headmistress remarked on how often a dull child seemed to gain intelligence when physical problems were remedied. Clearly, many children of perfectly normal intelligence were made to appear backward by reason of adenoids, malnutrition and poor sight, and they were able to gain enormously from this type of education, which was far more progressive than anything found in most of the normal elementary schools. The children had more space and more freedom and were not subject to harsh discipline.

The results must have seemed miraculous if teachers had considered these children of poor intelligence previously. Of course, all the children then attending elementary schcols would have benefited from such regimes!

Questions of hygiene and the suitability of school buildings for children's academic work also arose. Doctors became aware of the potential dangers schools held for the dissemination of infectious diseases. The lighting and ventilation of schools began to be taken into account. As newer schools were built, incorporating a variety of innovations, alternative curricula came into existence, creating a greater disparity, as Seaborne and Lowe pointed out:

> One commentator claimed in 1899 that there were at least six teaching systems currently used in English schools, varying from the one-teacher school at one extreme, to a complete adoption of classrooms at the other. Those still using schoolrooms with constant distractions arising from several groups working in the same room must have relied on firm discipline, rote methods of learning, with relatively few exchanges between teacher and individual child. In these situations it was difficult for the curriculum to extend far beyond the 'three Rs'. Those schools which adopted classroom teaching, and used dual desks rather than benches, were able to offer an education which was broader, if not radically different in character.

The discovery during the Boer War that a large number of young working-class men were of very poor physique was worrying to the government with its growing colonial commitments and led to the start of welfare provision in schools. Fresh air and physical exercise, as well as school meals and medical inspections, were seen to be necessary, especially to promote the physical development of boys who might one day be needed as soldiers and policemen. This concern, reinforced by the campaigning of teachers Rachel and Margaret McMillan, who opened 'camp schools' for poor children in the early 20th century, led to the building of open-air schools, which were set up by several local authorities in England. The McMillan sisters went on to open a nursery school which took children from 18 months to seven years, alone or with their mothers. The buildings, designed by Rachel, were light and easy to erect. They were open to the fresh air and were to influence the design of nursery and infant schools in the years to come.

Like the special schools, the open-air schools enabled teachers to develop a different kind of relationship with their pupils, and to experiment with a more open and child-centred curriculum. Another feature of schools built during this period was the marching corridor, designed to promote drill and improve physical development. The increase in the use of corridors in schools also allowed more movement within the school, something which was beginning to be thought desirable. The curriculum, after the final removal of the Revised Code, was beginning to change and there were signs of a move towards observation lessons in which children were more actively involved than before, because the ideas of Pestalozzi, Herbart, Froebel and Montessori were winning more adherents at all levels of education.

In 1914 the central hall plan was officially discarded and the Board of Education advocated 'single-storeyed groups of rooms, arranged to let the sun and air into every corner'. Classroom doors began to open directly into the fresh air. During the development of suburban buildings following the First World War, the veranda school became common in many areas, but these schools were a response to medical and hygienic considerations, rather than those of curriculum. During the 1930s the corridor school design became widespread, and at its most extreme became known as the 'finger-plan', with long rows of classrooms, separated by storage rooms, along corridors which led to cloakrooms, lavatories and washing facilities, all at some distance from the classrooms, as were the hall, dining space and school offices.

Neither the veranda schools, nor the finger-plan design, reflected the emphasis on activity methods which appeared in official statements, Again, according to Malcolm Seaborne:

> A study of the plans of schools actually built during the inter-war period, and of contemporary photographs of school interiors, suggests, however, that many of the recommendations about group work and more informal teaching methods remained theoretical, except in the nursery and more progressive infant and junior schools. The usual arrangement in infant and junior schools was to provide classrooms measuring 480 square feet and designed for 48 children arranged in four rows of dual desks with aisles between.

And this remained the norm until the advent of the Second World War in which 5,000 schools were damaged or destroyed.

Post-war design

The evacuation of children from all the major cities, which caused the sharing of innumerable country and small town schools, often developed new relationships between teachers and taught. Many teachers found themselves truly 'in loco parentis' and this led to less formal relationships in the classrooms. For those children left behind in the cities, frequent interruptions of teaching by air-raids and the sharing of dangers changed their relationships too. This might well have had an effect upon teacher attitudes. When the ranks of the teachers were swelled by large numbers of emergency-trained men and women from the Services, narrow views of education were inevitably challenged.

The 1944 Education Act specified more appropriate school build-ings and educational improvement. The immediate post-war years saw a sharp rise in the birth rate, and the building of many new housing estates with their attendant schools. There was a boom in school building and school design became a specialist concern. As Eric Pearson, HMI attached to the Architects and Building Branch at the Ministry of Education put it, in *Trends in School Design* in 1972:

> From 1950 onwards . . . there emerged in England a few groups of architects whose interests went a good deal beyond the application of their formal principles and practice to the design and building of primary schools. They came to realise that ideas about the education of young children were changing and that teachers were wanting to use their buildings differently from the way they had a few years before. Architecture is a social art, these architects were saying, and it begins with people; with the kind of school life they wish to create; with the new relationships between teachers and children; with the new ways of learning being explored.

Many of the young architects, attracted to school building and interested in new educational ideas, like many of the new teachers, were ex-servicemen and women. Many were also themselves the parents of young children and were affected by the ideas of popular democracy then current. Their own children would be attending maintained schools, unlike the children of professional families before the war, who had almost always received their education in the private sector. This may well have been another factor which stimulated the flowering of school design.

In 1949 the Ministry of Education reorganised its Architects and Building Branch and set up a Development Group within it. The brief for this group was to study and execute new developments in school building design. However, economic factors soon restricted its freedom and in 1950 a limit was put upon the cost per place allowed in the building of schools. The original cost limit for primary schools was £200 but this was reduced to £170 in 1950 and to £140 in 1951, although the cost of building rose in the same period. By 1971 it had risen to £257, although building costs by then had escalated rapidly. There were some who said that the cost-per-place limit had had a beneficial result. This point of view was put forward strongly in a Ministry of Education publication, *The Story of Post-War Building*, published in 1957, which maintained that the introduction of cost-per-place limits was giving value for money:

Early schools were extravagant of land and floor space. The next advance was therefore to reduce the total area without loss of physical standards and even with an increase in the amount of teaching space. Two principal means were used to this end.

First, all the unproductive non-teaching areas – mainly corridors – were cut down to a minimum. To remove the corridors from a finger-plan school is to remove the bone structure of the whole design. New designs were, therefore, produced that fundamentally altered the economics of school building.

Secondly, we came to realise that one space, suitably designed, could often do the work of two spaces. A corridor could be both a circulation area and part of a classroom. An entrance hall could also be a dining room. An assembly hall could be designed to serve as a gymnasium as well. By making a space serve two purposes we can reduce the total area without restricting the amount of variety of the facilities provided. So successful has this approach been that, during the last six years, the total area per child in primary schools has been cut by about 40 per cent.

Within the smaller total area, however, the amount of teaching space per child has been maintained or slightly increased.

This policy could be applied to our homes too; if we were all to make one space fulfil two functions, say, by eliminating bedrooms and all living in bed-sitters, this too would be more economical of space and would cost less. Or we could do without hall space, and have our front doors opening directly into the living space, as one finds in some of the cheapest working-class housing, built in the last century. We don't want such economical building, if we can avoid it, because it is less comfortable. In schools too, these double-function spaces have severe drawbacks. Having worked in schools with triple-function spaces – for example, the dining space, the assembly hall and the gymnasium all in the same area – I know the frustration felt by both teachers and kitchen staff when a PE lesson goes on slightly longer and the lunch tables have to be put out and laid more quickly than usual. In fact the children in such schools have to have their physical education times limited to meet the needs of other users of these shared spaces. Something else which was clearly not taken into account was the heavy burden placed upon teachers and their ancillary helpers who are continually having to put up and take down the apparatus which is used for PE in order to make the hall available for lunch.

The Ministry statement is not entirely accurate, in any case. Their own figures show that while in small infant schools the minimum area of teaching accommodation was increased by 60 square feet, and in medium-sized infant schools by 440 square feet, in the largest infant schools the accommodation in fact fell between the 1945 regulations and the 1954 regulations, by 176 square feet. And in junior schools, all categories of school lost space, 400 square feet in the smallest schools, 865 square feet for medium-sized schools, and 1,788 square feet in the largest – although these were improved in 1981 when new regulations increased the minimum teaching area in junior schools by 20 per cent. Malcolm Seaborne, who was Principal of Chester College of Higher Education, comments:

> How did it come about that, as so often in the past, the new stress on economy seemed to chime in perfectly with the educational and architectural ideas then current?

Recent trends

The past 30 years have seen three main styles of school design, all of which have been developed to stay within the imposed cost limits, rather than to meet any educational needs.

One style, that of the 'compact' school of the 1950s, has groups of classrooms – two, three, or four in number – with shared storage, toilet and cloakroom facilities and sometimes with shared practical areas. These would be grouped around one or two halls, used for gymnastics and dining, as well as for assemblies.

This style began to give way to the second type, the semi-open school, which, while retaining clearly-defined classroom areas, no longer closed them off completely but left one or two sides open, so that spaces flowed into one another; practical areas were shared, and cloakrooms and toilets were dispersed around the teaching areas. In some cases toilets actually led off the classroom spaces, which while convenient in one way, could prove unpleasantly smelly in hot weather. These schools often had some small rooms for group work, and quiet areas. Some were built in hexagonal or octagonal shapes, which provided more corners in classrooms.

During the last two decades, a third style has become more common: the open school in which, like the old schoolroom, all the classes can be viewed at a glance, divisions being created by units of furniture. These schools too have small group rooms, music rooms and shared practical areas, but the classrooms flow into each other.

In the first style teachers had the freedom to decide their teaching methods for themselves; adjoining classrooms allowed for both single class work and other combinations if desired, and shared practical areas meant some co-operation had to take place. The second style was also a flexible one because there was enough separation between classroom areas for different kinds of activities to go on in neighbouring spaces, yet two or more teachers could easily work as a team if this was wanted. But in the last type, which one might call the school compartment type, one begins to feel that the stated aims of the 1957 Ministry of Education have been completely subordinated to the financial restrictions, which have now become dominant.

While post-war primary schools have modern features in common – the single- or two-storey design, low ceilings which give a homely feel, interesting wall textures and bright colours, space to display children's work, all combining to produce a visually attractive building with an atmosphere of informality – this does not necessarily extend to the school curriculum. This may not be in keeping with the modern appearance of the school, but may still be based on out-moded educational theories. So too, an old building does not necessarily signify that the curriculum will be out of date. There can also be mismatch of the building and the aspirations of its staff. There are old schools in which walls have been knocked down and new schools in which partitions have been put up. A school staff can change completely in a period of ten years or so, and a new set of staff might feel unable to function efficiently in a building, which, while it met the requirements of the previous staff, is uncongenial to them.

In a 1967 symposium on school building, *The Primary School – an Environment for Education*, known as the Pilkington Report, one of the contributors (P.Manning) claims that architects have sometimes set out to shape the education in the schools which they designed:

> One or two cases are known where architects have deliberately (and presumably with the concurrence of the local education authority) so shaped classrooms that it has been found difficult, though not quite impossible, to arrange children in formal, blackboard-oriented patterns. The building designs appear to have forced teachers, willy-nilly, to adopt the practice of teaching small, informal groups. Whether it is right for one profession to direct the way in which another works, even if their present ways seem bad, is doubtful.

I would not have thought that this was one of the key problems for the teaching profession at present. More to the point is the view put by another contributor to the Pilkington Report, Harold Hayling, who was then a member of the ILEA Inspectorate:

> A major hindrance to the development of new practices in primary education is the existence of a large number of old, cramped buildings, all too often inherited from secondary schools whose pupils have moved on to new buildings. Very often new buildings for primary schools make no concessions in their

planning to newer concepts of teaching, to the advent of technological change which has long since affected life outside the school. The result may be that traditional methods of teaching are reinforced by unimaginative planning of school buildings and teachers are trapped into perpetuating traditional teaching because of lack of space and facilities.

This is even more true in 1987 than it was in 1967. The recent increase in the birth rate in some areas has produced more young children for the present inadequate number of school places. These are fewer than they were because a few years ago a fall in rolls led to closure of some primary schools. Yet we still hear of the projected closure of small schools in various places. It seems that small is no longer beautiful. Unfortunately the schools are not elastic, they cannot expand and contract in order to accommodate the changes in numbers. Overcrowding in primary schools is in danger of returning once more, in some parts of the country.

Most teachers do their best, and many do amazing work in buildings which are not well designed for their ends. The best-designed schools are a joy for both children and staff to work in. It is quite clear that the design of school buildings and the facilities provided within them are crucial to the potential curriculum of the school within. Staff and children need space in which to work without interfering in the work of other classes. Schools need plenty of storage space and space for practical activities. Too much cost-cutting may well be a false economy in the long run because a school which lacks such facilities may prove to be a straitjacket which wears down teachers by making it difficult for them to extend the curriculum. The responsibility for this, however, rests on local and national government policy and financing, for the architect can only work to instructions.

When teachers and architects co-operate

Talking to a colleague recently, I discovered that he had been deputy head of a school, in another part of London, during the period when the school was being rebuilt. The staff were working in an old building, but were team-teaching. They had removed doors in the old school in order to make it more flexible for their organisation. When the new building was being planned, there were full discussions between teachers and architect, models were made,

Lego was used to discover the possibilities of the new building. The architect had been given limits to which he had to work; there were suggestions from the teachers which the architect could not carry out; there were suggestions from the architect which the teachers could not accept as being suitable for their educational purposes. But the co-operation finally provided those teachers with a building which closely matched their way of working, except that there was far less space than they had been used to in their old building. In order to meet the demands of the teachers, the architect cut costs on fittings, handles, window latches, etc. The school had several unusual features. The headteacher's room had two doors, one leading in from the entrance lobby, and the other, on the opposite wall, giving directly into the staffroom, something which would be an advantage in many other schools. Teaching areas were small, but all connected with common practical areas. The chief problem was lack of adequate storage space, which resulted from an overall shortage of space available on the site.

If when new schools are being planned, more consultation with teachers and parents could be built into the procedure, this would be very valuable. In my own school, the entrance was too narrow to accommodate pushchairs and prams safely. Yet we wanted parents to come into the school and into the classrooms: it was surely wrong that they had to leave sleeping infants unattended in their prams in order to do so. Disabled parents had to see teachers on the ground floor, although the school had three storeys. Ideally there would be ramps or lifts to enable parents to have full access to school buildings. Clearly this would impose extra costs, but since it is the parents, grandparents and other relatives of the children in the schools who contribute to the cost of school buildings, there should be more room for their participation in deciding what features should be included. School buildings should be designed to enhance the curriculum; a well-designed school is, after all, an effective school.

15 | Progressive means making progress

The history of education is full of incidents in which those who were considered 'progressive' had to battle against the status quo. There is ample evidence that developmental work has been carried out in maintained as well as fee-paying schools since their inception and that this work has been supported by many of HM Inspectors throughout the years. But it is a misconception to assume that a developmental or progressive curriculum is one without structure or discipline. The progressive curriculum is one which is searching for better ways of assisting children's progress.

However, there have been those situations where teachers have seen themselves as 'progressive', and have adopted certain manifestations of what they have perceived as progressive education, without studying or analysing the underlying structures. This is rather like rearranging the top soil without doing any digging: it may look different on the surface but a little investigation demonstrates that no-one has bothered to carry out the necessary labour without which real improvement cannot come about. This has led to numerous contradictions in their practice, a certain kind of sloppiness and lack of development in the curriculum. It has also provided ammunition for those who oppose progressive education; some of whom are on the left, seeing it as serving the interests of middle-class at the expense of working-class children; and some of whom are on the right, calling for a return to the maintenance tradition.

Progressives and pseudo-progressives

Two sociologists, Sharp and Green, who spent a year studying a self-styled progressive school which they called 'Mapledene', published a damning indictment of the school in 1975. They came to the conclusion that the school's failure to promote effective learning was not only being excused by progressivism, but was actually built

179

into the system. They described teachers who openly displayed prejudice against children who did not conform, and who were remarkably unself-critical. If to be progressive in education is to be part of the developmental tradition, there must be evidence of a developing curriculum in a school before it can be called 'progressive' in any way, however its teachers might like to view themselves.

A well-known instance of this kind developed in the 1970s in the William Tyndale Junior School in Islington (formerly Sebbon Street School). Since this was quite close to my own school, and since I was friendly with teachers on the staff of the infant school, it was familiar to me. When I was a deputy head, my headteacher, Frank Gray, had invited me to work with him and with the then head of the William Tyndale junior school, Alan Head, and the head of the infant school, Brenda Hart, on mathematics guidelines for primary children. In the course of this collaboration I became familiar with both of the schools. When Alan Head left, this kind of project was no longer possible.

Because it became a *cause célèbre* and attracted a great deal of media attention, there was considerable alarm among parents – and satisfaction to Black Paperites, because it was presented as a dispute about progressive education. This was another case where a staff claimed to be 'progressive' but made no attempt to introduce appropriate structures or even to define their curriculum, let alone involve themselves in curriculum development. Like the Mapledene staff, they were completely unself-critical and tried to use progressivism as an excuse for a kind of woolly approach which led them into such difficulties with parents, school managers and neighbouring teachers that they were involved in a public inquiry (conducted by Robin Auld QC) and, finally, dismissed from the teaching service.

They were in fact much concerned with yet another dichotomy: could schools be agencies of social change or must they be agencies of social control? This appeared to have priority in their discussions, as reported to the Inquiry. Staff meetings provided a forum where this question was discussed at length, causing practical decisions about the curriculum to be shelved indefinitely:

> The staff discussions during this term did not lead to a single collective decision of any significance relating to the educational aims or organisation or teaching methods to be adopted in

the school. They degenerated early on into a series of heated philosophical debates in which the discussion ranged from the subject of teaching methods to more fundamental questions such as the functions of schools in society and the structure of society itself, its evils and the need for changes. (*William Tyndale Junior and Infants Schools Public Inquiry Report*)

Unfortunately, the media, showing complete ignorance of the issues involved, insisted on falsely equating the happenings at this school with 'progressive' and 'modern' methods. Yet in evidence to the Inquiry it was clearly stated by parents and managers that their criticisms were not about progressive or traditional methods, but that the teachers could not be said to be teaching by any method.

The teachers saw themselves as a collective: but so do the staffs of many schools. The difference, perhaps, lies in the fact that these teachers seemed to be so concerned with their own rights and with confrontation with any form of authority that they were either unaware or uncaring of the effects of their policies, or lack of policies, on those around them, including their pupils. The teachers at William Tyndale fell into the trap of regarding teachers' rights as something distinct from and overriding the rights of the children. Such a stance would inevitably lead to problems, for schools exist for the education of children, and while teachers must have decent pay and conditions, their interests cannot take precedence over those of the children. Further, such a position can only antagonise parents with whom teachers need to be in partnership in order to achieve a better education for their children.

That there were instances of non-teaching, and even non-supervision, of children was clear: teachers were frequently called away for staff meetings:

As the year wore on, nearly every time Mr Ellis [the headteacher] had an official visitor, Mr Haddow, the mainstay of his team of four, would leave his corridor post and be in there with the head and his visitor taking notes. (*William Tyndale: Collapse of a School or a System?* Gretton and Jackson)

Brian Haddow had introduced an options system, as he explained in his evidence:

Terry Ellis and I had many educational discussions and after the half-term we decided that the school would need to develop in a different way if it were to meet the demands of all the children. It was agreed that I could develop a wider approach to the curriculum with my fourth-year class. With the children I decided on a range of 20 activities to be set up for them. They had the choice to move freely to the one they wished to do. I expanded these activities from the classroom into the hall outside.

Such an ambitious programme would need detailed planning and the co-operation of the entire staff. It would require a tremendous amount of work and discussion both before and after school to ensure that the equipment and books which might be needed were available. It would also require constant intervention by teachers to ensure that the quality of the children's learning experiences was good, and monitoring by teachers to ensure that children's time was not being wasted. This would be a monumental task when the children were scattered around the school. Even more so when, as the report made clear, there were frequent staff absences, when Mr Haddow regarded his attendance at the headteacher's discussions as having priority over his teaching commitments, and there was a slackness of attitude on the part of many staff, which 'manifested itself in their frequent late arrival to work in the mornings and the afternoons'. Since one of the tenets of true progressive education is the role of the adults as models for the learners, one can only wonder what such behaviour by the teachers was supposed to convey to the children. It is hardly surprising that 'indiscipline became one of the major problems of the Junior School'.

In their own book, *William Tyndale: The Teachers' Story*, the teachers do not give an account of the curriculum as they saw it. The book divides between generalities and a detailed history of their differences with the school managers. They claimed that they saw themselves as providing for the most deprived children and giving their needs priority. How this could be equated with leaving those children with greater needs and fewer resources than their peers unsupervised and undirected, is difficult to understand. Teachers were working hard in the schools around the area of Tyndale, to ensure that children who were coping with severe problems, of whatever kind, received extra support, discussing children's problems with their parents and getting advice from other professionals. Yet these schools were accused by the Tyndale teachers of operating a kind of 'dustbin' policy. This is strange terminology since, to walk into the William Tyndale Junior School at that time was to enter an environment which was itself becoming dangerously close to a dustbin. Again, what impression can the pupils have gained of the junior teachers' view of them when they compared the junior school environment with that of the infant school they had attended downstairs? The Inspectors' reports quoted at the Auld Inquiry contrast the appearance and educational impact of the two schools:

The infant school

An environment that is welcoming, domestic in atmosphere, interesting to children and full of colour. Tiles are covered with bright washable wallpaper, children's painting and writing are well mounted and displayed, there are small displays of pictures and natural objects related to current interests and plants are provided by the school and tended by the children. The total impression in the corridors and in the hall is of an environment that children contribute to, use and enjoy. Above all it is impossible to be unaware of books.

An environment of this kind has not only to be created; it has to be maintained and renewed. The two infants' helpers take pride in painting, repairing and generally caring for the environment in each room in turn and in the school as a whole. The school-keeper and his staff co-operate fully in maintaining a high standard of care and cleanliness in the school. Inside the classrooms the teachers create an environment that reflects and provokes interest and where materials are organised in such a way that children can reach and replace them easily. Each teacher has made an effort to make her classroom visually interesting and intellectually stimulating.

This is a picture which will be familiar to many parents with children in good primary schools. But contrast it with the following description:

The junior school

If the condition of the school environment at the time of the visit is typical, then it is clear that environmentally the children enter into a different world when transferring from the infant school to the junior. The approach to the junior department is along stairways of dark brown glazed brickwork. Display space in the corridor is limited by the size of the boards available, but even these, small as they are, were completely empty. Attempts had indeed been made to cover the brown and green tiles at the bottom of the walls with various oddments of wallpaper, but any enhancing effect had been destroyed by the rough treatment the paper has had. The upstairs hall was indescribably bitty with a confusion of drama apparatus and library shelves, a portable coat hanger, a piano and two or three bedraggled items of display . . . apart from the room where the deputy teaches . . . and one other room the display of visual material was restricted in range and quality. There were no nature or interest tables.

Of the other specialist rooms and the school in general as seen through an art inspector's eye, the following was written:

The art room in which I taught for two afternoons is a barren desert; there are no paintings on the walls and there is no reference material in the room of any description. The paint and materials have to be fetched from a store cupboard at the end of the corridor. The school is lucky to have the facility of an art room, but in no visible way has it been exploited. It should be full of visual stimuli in the form of plants, man-made objects, natural forms and photographic reference materials. The walls should be covered in pinboard and the tables should be prepared with separate powder colour, palettes, water pots and brushes.

A working atmosphere in a school is brought about by the thought, care and pride which is put into the enrichment of the children's environment. Here the school has little to offer.

Other inspectors found a similar situation. A classroom contained:

A small badly-damaged collection of books . . . There was nothing else usable . . . There were no readers, no apparatus, no art materials and none of the valuable and common stimulating equipment that a primary classroom usually holds.

The library shelves in the hall were in such a jumble that it was difficult to distinguish their contents, and equipment and furniture were heaped among them as to make them almost impossible to use . . . the absence of a central library of any significance . . . shows a disregard for the provision of reading material capable of helping those able to use it.

It is difficult to see how the teachers' claim to be giving priority to the children most in need could have been maintained when the school was so depressing and chaotic. They claimed in their book a philosophy, the aim of which was to 'exercise positive discrimination towards the disadvantaged'. The disadvantaged are said to be the working-class, poor and immigrant pupils. It seems to me that if the staff claimed they were giving priority to these pupils, they were showing them and their families a grave lack of respect by giving them such a slovenly environment. Did they suppose that it was only the middle classes that preferred clean, bright and well-kept schools? Another question which arises is why a group of middle-class teachers should regard the children of middle-class professionals, like themselves, as being in some way undeserving of their teachers' professional care.

Strangely, for a group which considered itself so radical, under pressure from parents worried about lack of progress in their children's reading they proceeded to divide the whole junior school into streamed ability groups. This would be seen as a very dubious undertaking by progressive teachers who regard streaming as a kind of self-fulfilling prophecy, and a counter-productive exercise. This was certainly not a form of organisation to be found in a progressive school. The reading groups were abandoned before long because, to quote again from the Auld Report:

The scheme was not planned properly. If more than one member of the staff was absent, the entire reading groups for the day were cancelled. No arrangements were made for re-allocation for the day to other reading groups of children from reading groups whose teacher was away.

Some members of the staff did not always use the reading group sessions to teach reading or language skills, but allowed the children to follow other activities . . . Some members of the staff had little experience or knowledge of how to conduct reading groups . . . [they] had not been very methodical in preparing themselves for this new scheme of teaching language skills.

It cannot be said too often that this dispute had nothing whatever to do with progressive education. It was an experiment in teacher power and appeared to be attempting to elevate laziness into an educational philosophy. Its chief importance now is that it is still dragged in by the education spokespersons and the media from time to time and used to attack progressive ideas which governments might find too expensive!

As to whether schools are agencies for social control or social change, I would say that they fulfil both functions, have been used for both purposes at various times, and are capable of being used in both ways at one and the same time. Arguing about their dominant role is less productive than ensuring that all children are as well equipped as possible to make the wisest choices in their personal and political lives, and that education is a positive and enjoyable experience for our children.

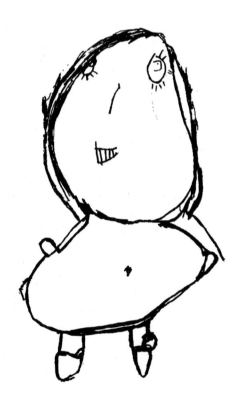

16 | Those move easiest who have learned to dance

Just as there is no simple either-or solution to the question of whether schools are in fact agencies for social control, or for social change, so, many of the other dichotomies which plague teachers cannot be simplistically resolved. Laurie Buxton has argued, as did Herbart, that what a student *feels* is as important as what he or she thinks, and that this even applies in mathematics, thought by many to be a purely intellectual subject. Perhaps other dichotomies should also be examined for the connections between them. Neither the progressive nor the maintenance traditions can, in themselves, be a guarantee of high standards; those depend on other factors.

Formal/informal

The formal versus informal controversy overlooks the fact that there are formal occasions even in informal schools. Schools are more or less eclectic and there is a range of behaviours suitable for different occasions. School assemblies, concerts or theatrical performances require more formal behaviour than does the classroom; otherwise they could not be enjoyed by anyone. Many of the events I have attended in my own schools and in others have been more disturbed by noise from the adults in the audience than from children.

Probably the most regimented and formal procedures in any school are fire drills, where absolute silence and obedience are vital. This is understood to be necessary for the safety of those involved, by all concerned, down to the youngest children, who realise that in a fire, noise, confusion, self-expression of any kind could result in injury or death. Any activity which involves physical danger demands silence and concentration, and this applies to physical education too. Even in a classroom silence is appropriate when all are listening to one member, whether that member is a teacher or a child. If a school does not encourage children to adapt their behaviour to circumstances, either by allowing every child to speak all the time so that no-one learns to listen, or by demanding silence from everyone except the teacher, the effect may be to mask all kinds of underground activity and boredom. Nor can such a school be said to be educating its pupils fully.

My experience of some informal occasions in schools, such as children's Christmas parties, or school-leaving parties, has taught me that these have to be very well organised and have a clear and agreed structure. To leave such occasions perfectly 'free' is a recipe for disaster and tears. Any parent who has hosted a child's birthday party will understand this apparent contradiction.

Child or subject centred?

Here again an either-or approach can be limiting educationally. Child-centred education, properly planned, demands the selection of experiences which are most appropriate to the child's conceptual stage and to the particular activity being undertaken. In early childhood the child's own experience is the best starting point from which to extend interest and understanding. As that extension takes place, and the child matures and becomes curious about specific subject areas, some degree of subject teaching then becomes appropriate to the child's mode of thought. There must, though, still be opportunities for pupils to investigate the connections *between* subjects and make personal reconstructions in areas of study. It is often the rigid demarcation lines between subjects which prove counter-productive in education. But completely child-centred education, such as that practised on Emile, who had a personal tutor, is impossible in large classes, as the ORACLE research shows.

Concentration on the child's own experience, without a concurrent emphasis on extending that experience by every means possible, can lead to a trivialisation of education, and its confinement to the immediate environment, whereas education should extend that environment and make the whole world the concern of every child.

Grammar or not?

Official concern about whether or not to teach parts of speech and language structures exemplify this either-or view of education. Kenneth Baker, Education Secretary, set up a committee of enquiry, early in 1987, to advise on the development of a model of the language for use in schools, but its membership did not include anyone actually teaching primary age children and this may well prove a serious omission, because what is being done in many primary schools now is very relevant to this concern.

If early teaching, based on developmental writing, as described in Chapter 6, is appropriate to the more concrete mode of thinking found in younger children, then more advanced modes of thought will be capable of dealing with more sophisticated aspects of language. It is the provision of *appropriate* experience which will assist the development from the concrete or enactive stage into the more abstract iconic phase, and ultimately, again with relevant experience, into the symbolic system of thought. The child who does not have access to the necessary early experiences may have much greater difficulty in passing out of the concrete stage, but this is not always understood by those without experience of work with the very young. Nor may they be familiar with the findings of researchers like Piaget and Bruner.

Until the child has reached a more advanced stage, the teaching of parts of speech would be a formal exercise which would not be fully understood by the student. The teacher's role is the analysis of the student's level and provision of the kinds of experiences most appropriate to the student's needs at different stages. To attempt to teach formal structures to pupils before they have sufficient language experience, whatever their age, would in no way serve to accelerate their progress in developing good language strategies.

It is always necessary to bear in mind that we do return to more concrete thought processes when tackling new concepts. As Bruner has said, it is possible to teach anything usefully, at some level, to children at different ages. So when we talk about teaching parts of speech, this can be done earlier with some children who read fluently and have developed an interest in and feeling for language. Children with a wide experience of print will often be able to define a sentence at the age of six, stating that it begins with a capital letter and ends with a full stop. This has meaning for them because they have had the sight of many sentences in their reading. But it would not have the same meaning for a six-year-old who had not yet begun to read. At seven, many children can begin to make sets of nouns and verbs, being able to perceive the distinction between 'naming' and 'doing', and can begin to recognise adjectives and adverbs. But this will vary according to the language experience of the children concerned, and nothing would be more wasteful than teaching parts of speech to the child who was only just beginning to read!

There are points in language education at which the teaching of language structures is useful because the learner is beginning to use more advanced constructions and their identity soon becomes apparent. This knowledge is then illuminating and can be linked with what is already known about language in the mind of the learner, thus forming a coherent scheme which, because it is understood, can be remembered. This is not the case when learning is by rote: this is drudgery rather than illumination.

There is certainly a point at which some language forms which have dropped out of use cease to be taught, except in so far as they are of historical interest. Language is constantly in the process of change and has always been so. If there had been no changes we would all still be using 'thee' and 'thou' and the word 'presently' would mean 'now', instead of 'in the near future'.

Structure is, *per se*, implicit in any form of organisation. Without rules and limits there is only chaos. The argument is really about how these are best acquired by young learners. Should they be taught didactically, whether or not they can be understood by the students, or should teachers provide a wide range of such selected experiences which would facilitate the children's learning and enable them to generalise the rules for themselves? In chapter 7 I referred to the difference between instrumental and relational understanding, and this is another facet of that same argument.

Perhaps the difficulties suffered by so many of the adolescents who are so often referred to as being unable to write or spell properly have arisen because they did not have access to sufficient first-hand experience in their early learning and have never been able to develop out of their early learning stages and integrate into their internal mental structures the rote learning they were given. Progressive teachers do not say that children should not be helped to spell correctly, merely that they do not think that frequent and competitive spelling tests are the best way to encourage this learning.

Structure and freedom are inseparable

Without structure there can be no freedom, only anarchy. In order to have a classroom in which a child has freedom to explore, it must be carefully structured. First and foremost, children must be safe in schools. Then the materials for exploration must be organised and made available. The children themselves need help in learning to organise their time and to recognise the limitations imposed by the classroom situation. A child may be free to explore avenues of learning, to experiment with the equipment available, to make mistakes, but not to do anything he or she pleases, regardless of its effect on others.

Supporting pupils in the process of learning how to use the opportunities available and how to exercise choice is best taught by adults providing role models. The example of the teacher is all-important, nowhere more so than in the area of self-control. Perhaps the only forms of control – one component of education – which have intrinsic value are those which lead to self-control, which has to be practised in order to develop. Children need behaviour models presented by adults who demonstrate self-control. This is one powerful argument against corporal punishment.

School discipline which depends upon hierarchical authority structures and external incentives and constraints – for example, a prefect system – will not assist pupils towards self-control. It is only when pupils are involved in learning which *they* recognise as productive for themselves, and which provides intrinsic satisfaction, that they become willing to accept the limits laid down by the school. This willingness, which implies the active co-operation of the pupils, grows from the understanding that it is necessary to control one's behaviour in society in order that all may benefit. Problems arise when pupils have not learned to exercise control over themselves, either through an absence of good models, or through lack of opportunity to practise because they have always been controlled by external authority. And problems also arise when pupils do not feel that they have access to a curriculum which offers intrinsic satisfaction.

As those move easiest who have learned to dance

In order to have an effective and informal school which offers maximum freedom to its pupils, it must be highly structured and well organised. While this may seem contradictory it is no more so than the fact that the most ethereal-seeming ballet dancers are those with the strongest muscles and the most highly-developed technique, built painstakingly through long hours of practice. As Alexander Pope wrote in *An Essay on Criticism*:

> True ease in writing comes from art, not chance
> As those move easiest who have learned to dance.

Visitors to primary classrooms which appear very informal may wonder how it is possible that all those small children are moving around, largely amicably, intent on their business, without any evidence of organisation. Such classrooms require the most complex structures and detailed organisation. Like a beautifully-performed ballet, they come about through art; in this case it is the art of the teacher, and, like that of the ballet dancer, it is based on many hours of painstaking practice.

Since children in schools are learning social behaviour, among other things, there are bound to be false moves and mistakes, misbehaviour of various kinds. Such mistakes have to be expected, but they also have to be pointed out as inappropriate, and if they are not self-corrected, some need to be prevented because they may be potentially dangerous to others. It is the responsibility of the adults involved with them to minimise the consequences of such mistakes and experiments. This is easier to do within a tightly-controlled and formal organisation. Once children begin to move around a classroom or school informally, as individuals or in small groups, oversight becomes more difficult and demands more of teachers in time and commitment.

Learning takes place both inside and outside classrooms; much of it happens on staircases, and in corridors and playgrounds and a lot of that learning may be negative (i.e. children learning to behave in anti-social ways). Prefect systems have been used to fill the gap caused by too few available adults, just as once pupil teachers filled similar gaps. Perhaps the reason why so many formal schools still exist is that this does enable some kind of control to be exercised where the ratio of adults to children is too low for more desirable forms of control to be instituted. Control rooted in self-discipline is more costly to achieve, though it is more valuable and more effective. The first and most basic requirement for its achievement is a much better ratio of adults to children than has yet been contemplated.

17 | Resources or resourcefulness?

It has frequently been stated by Secretaries of State for Education that improvements in education should occur through better management of resources, and not be dependent upon increased finance. Resources is the term used to describe all the people and equipment needed in the schools. Human resources are the teaching and non-teaching staffs; there are technical resources such as typewriters, science equipment, computers; and library resources, or books, charts and posters. Schools use specialised equipment for mathematics and language work, and these are part of the school's resources. The paper, pencils, paint, glue, craft materials used are consumable resources. All these resources have one thing in common – they cost money for schools to acquire.

There has been great concern expressed, in secondary schools and elsewhere, about the introduction of the new GCSE examination without necessary resources. Is the official view correct? Do schools have adequate resources which just need to be properly organised? It seems not, according to Wigan headteacher, Dick Williams:

> The criteria insist that experiments done in groups are no longer acceptable; the pupil has to do it himself. That means you need 20 sets of equipment. (*The Times Educational Supplement* 5 September 1986)

Since his school was only equipped with single sets for demonstration purposes, the new requirements necessitate a considerable outlay on science equipment which will be impossible without additional finance being made available.

This headteacher's view is echoed in the findings of HMI who recently conducted an inspection of education in Wigan. They reported that the quality of education was such that Wigan was generally well-placed to respond constructively and effectively to future educational needs, but added that doing so would involve some increase in its spending on education. So it does not seem that that problem *can* be solved simply by 'managing better'. Expenditure is necessary so that pupils can get what is now called 'hands-on' experience, which is being promoted as if it is a new idea. Of course it is not; it is our old friend first-hand experience called by another name suggestive of technological advance. If our schools had been financed and organised so that all pupils at both primary and secondary levels had in the past had adequate opportunities for the most extensive first-hand experience, this sudden revolution would not have been required.

If government resources for education have to be so strictly limited that schools have been making do with one set of equipment where 20 were needed, it is truly remarkable that tens of millions are siphoned off to support fee-paying schools, both through the assisted places scheme – which provides government-funded independent school places for bright children – and through the tax concessions granted to those with charitable status. Recent research has shown the former to have failed to fulfil the stated aims for which it was set up, as reported in *The Guardian* of 4 September 1986.

According to a four-year study by a team of researchers from Bristol Polytechnic and Newcastle University, funded by the Economic and Social Research Council (a quango), most pupils on the scheme have come from middle-class backgrounds and the researchers concluded that the scheme 'has not attracted in large numbers the kinds of pupils from inner-city areas or manual working-class backgrounds who figured so heavily in the imagery employed by ministers at the time of its introduction'.

The report goes on to say that a significant minority of the pupils in the assisted places scheme would have gone to independent schools without it! Thus the scheme is subsidising their parents at the tax-payers' expense and at a cost to the vast majority of the nation's children. If we are to have a dual system of schools, and if there are parents wealthy enough to pay school fees, then surely they should do so, without the gift of money from those who are far less well off, and whose children are being deprived of the most elementary school equipment by education cuts.

Few in education would deny that management could be improved, and numerous courses have been devised to help those with responsibilities in schools to improve their management skills. But management training itself is expensive in terms of time and re-placement staff for those on courses. There has always been a great deal of 'spoiling the ship for a ha'p'orth of tar' in the field of education because very few good ideas are without implementation costs, and many necessary improvements are not made because someone holding the purse strings decides they are too costly to pursue. Since education does not produce an outcome which can be realised as a measurable profit, investment in it seems unattractive to government until public pressure forces an increased input. This is inevitably too little and too late.

Action in defence of education

There have been many criticisms of teachers for taking the action they have. But look at their alternative. Should they with brave smiles have continued to work with diminishing resources, in badly run-down schools, all on inadequate pay? It is not merely the teachers who have suffered from shortage of equipment; above all, it has been the children whose education was being damaged, long before the action began. Can anyone doubt that the present public focus on education and the widespread agreement that it is under-resourced, would have come about without the teachers' action? To quote from *Hamlet*:

Whether 'tis nobler in the mind to suffer
The slings and arrows of outrageous fortune,
Or to take arms against a sea of troubles,
And by opposing end them?

Criticisms levelled at teachers for taking action when all other channels had been tried (HMI reports over many years have warn-ed governments about deteriorating conditions in schools through-out the country) would be better directed at the governments which have for so long used the teachers as scapegoats for the situation in the schools, which has been brought about by the policies of those very governments.

One of the issues highlighted by the teachers' campaign has been the practice of teachers being asked to cover lessons for absent colleagues. If the planning and preparation of lessons and the marking of pupils' work is a vital part of teaching, then some time needs to be allowed for this during the school day. This has generally been allowed in secondary schools, but not in primary schools, although it has often been agreed that it was necessary.

Why do teachers so dislike this task? Because it takes away precious preparation time, time which they expected to devote to their own work. Free periods are not free time in which no work needs to be done; they are provision for part of the teaching task, the preparation of lessons and the marking of pupils' work. For some teachers they provide essential time in which to perform a special responsibility post. Teachers become over-tired and feel frustrated because their own work has not been well enough prepared, or because they have to renege on commitments made – to give extra tuition to a pupil or visit the class of a junior colleague, to give advice.

But there is no easy solution to this problem. To have a force of supply teachers large enough to meet any contingency in the schools is probably impossible to achieve. During an influenza epidemic schools in a particular authority might be reduced to two-thirds of their normal staffing. The authority might need to provide 200 or more supply teachers in such a situation. Yet three months later the demand would have fallen to perhaps an average of 45 or 50 per week. Various attempts have been made to solve this problem but none has been effective because the numbers of teachers likely to fall ill in any period cannot be predicted. Most teachers have the common sense to understand this, but it is when they feel they are severely underpaid and undervalued that requests to cover prove to be the last straw.

What can be predicted, however, is how many teachers will be out of their schools on courses and related matters, and on long-term absences, like maternity leave, and these should always be adequately covered. This approach has certainly been used within the ILEA, where for some time all daytime in-service training has been given priority supply cover. It is where authorities, in order to stay within government limits, restrict the size of the supply teacher force that conditions will be worst.

Another prediction which can be made is that as teachers' conditions worsen, so the incidence of illness increases. An improvement in conditions of work and a lessening of the frustration felt by teachers might well lower the demand for supply cover and lessen teachers' anger on those occasions when requests to cover for an absent colleague are unavoidable.

One gain that has been made, however, is the employment of separate staff to supervise the period of the lunch break. This does at least enable teachers to have a short rest, or even to do some of their work, while the children are having their break. When teachers were expected to supervise they very often had to decide between preparing for their afternoon's work or having lunch themselves.

Should teachers pay?

There have been countless comparisons of teachers' pay with that of comparable professions, and it is quite clear that they are poorly paid, and remain so, even after recent pay increases. Sir Keith Joseph, when Education Secretary, always maintained that so long as schools were adequately staffed and there were enough recruits entering the teaching profession there was no need to make any substantial improvement to teachers' salaries. But this argument does not take into account the numbers of long-serving teachers and headteachers retiring early – thus diminishing the level of experience in the profession – and the numbers of younger teachers 'escaping' into other careers, or moving into better-paid teaching jobs abroad. Teachers' pay is reckoned to part of the total education budget and so long as any rise in salaries is balanced against a fall in the rest of education funding – a form of blackmail – teachers are being asked to pay for equipping and maintaining the schools *out of their own pockets*. Money which should be paid to them in salaries is having to be used to resource the schools in order to save LEA and government finance – some of which, like the assisted places scheme, is of no benefit to the vast majority of children, their parents or their teachers.

An unexpected ally is Professor Brian Cox, a member of the committee of enquiry into English language teaching, and one of the editors of the *Black Papers*, which introduced a backlash against progressive ideas during the 1970s. Writing about the evils of youth unemployment in *The Times Educational Supplement* (1 November 1985), he spoke for many:

> The greatest weakness of this government is that it has not invested enough money in education . . . How will these ventures be paid for? Under the Conservative government spending on

defence has increased by 20 per cent in real terms. Money must
be transferred from the defence budget to education.

Millions of parents and teachers will agree with Professor Cox.
There is a need for investment at all levels of education. The
situation which faces so many school-leavers now, with both jobs
and further education places limited, is one which has a domino
effect on the education of those still at school. If there is no
opportunity to use the skills acquired, they lose the incentive to
learn. Radical changes are needed to provide them with the opportunities to which they have a right.

It is this desire for radical change which lies behind the campaigning by the teachers. Unfortunately the teachers' unions
allowed themselves to be divided, which facilitated government
intervention and led to the teachers being diverted from their main
aim, which was to bring about advances in the schools as well as
in teachers' pay and conditions. It remains true, however, that such
a long-overdue improvement on both fronts is a vital part of any
general advance. No country can have a healthy, confident and
efficient education service with a grossly underpaid and overworked teaching force.

An easy job?

People who have little contact with schools, and who retain a
pupil's-eye view of teaching, may think that teachers work from
9am to 4pm and have long holidays, and, though they will concede
that the pay is poor, justify this by the seemingly short hours. An
ex-teacher, Paul Davies (who is now working abroad), gives a more
realistic picture in *The Times Educational Supplement* (5
September 1986):

> My working week now appears to be significantly longer than
> my teaching hours. Yet all the things that I did in my own time
> are now part of the working week. Management meetings,
> hitherto always after school, are now scheduled as an important
> part of my work. Planning is not only a requirement but seen
> as the corner-stone of successful work. I am still expected to
> keep abreast of developments and standards in my field − but
> in company time. When I leave work, my time is my own. I do
> not spend nearly 20 hours a week marking at home. In fact,

when I work overtime, I get paid for it. . .

So when the English people at work tell me that I must notice the difference between working and teaching, you can see why I smile. Teaching was far harder work than anything I am required to do now.

An account of the work of a primary teacher comes from *The Making of the Primary School* by Jan Stewart:

> Teaching itself has always been a high-pressure task. Any parent knows what it is like having two children in the house on a wet Saturday. Imagine three friends being invited for the day. Would not this add to the pressure? Then think of a child you would rather not have to tea. In your mind's eye, picture identical twins with the same characteristics turning up to join the group. Think of organising them and disciplining them for a whole day. Are you becoming tired just contemplating it? A teacher does not have twice as much to cope with, her or his pressure is at least four times as great from Monday to Friday, week in, week out. There is also the added stress of not just containing and occupying the group, but educating them.

Nor are the teacher's hours short: a 1971 survey by Hilsum and Cane, *The Teacher's Day*, showed that the average primary teacher worked a 44.25 hour week, which, even after adjustments for holidays, still averaged 38.2 hours per week. Since 1971 the workload has increased considerably and many teachers with whom I have worked are in school at 8 or 8.30am and are still there at 5.30 or 6pm. These times are extended when they attend parents' evenings, governors' meetings, curriculum and staff meetings, or help at sales, or are involved with sports or school journeys. These teachers are usually in their schools for part of their school holidays, and work at home as well. They look for books and equipment for their classrooms during weekends and holidays and, when school funds are low, sometimes pay for these themselves.

Who will pay Baker's Bill?

How could a Secretary of State in a country which claims to be a democracy propose a Bill which would end all consultation with professional bodies, deny any rights of salary negotiation between employers and employed and may well break international conventions? If Mr Baker had the aim of maintaining unrest and demoralisation among teachers, he could have found no better method. He gave his reasons in his speech to the House of Commons on the occasion of the Second Reading of the Teachers' Pay and Conditions Bill. Among them was the need to end the kind of 'negotiating brawl' of the past two years. This completely ignores the fact that the problems in negotiations arose because the government stubbornly refused to allocate adequate finance to education. In some ways education has been made 'piggy-in-the-middle' in the political battle between national and local government. In its desire to control local government, the national government made it virtually impossible for local authorities to offer adequate salaries to their teachers. In all this the needs of the children going through the education system now have been cynically ignored.

The effects of the Bill will be to worsen teachers' conditions of work – and parents should note that it must inevitably also worsen children's conditions of learning, something which is usually over-looked. Since there has been no stated limit on class size, very large classes are likely to return, especially as the Bill contained no measures for increasing the supply of teachers. This is a disastrously retrogressive step for children who will be affected. Further, teachers could be called upon to provide unlimited cover for absent colleagues, and there is no allowance for teachers to have time out of class to prepare lessons and mark work, or support colleagues. A whole range of duties which have been voluntary will become contractual. Teachers could, for example, be called upon to attend unspecified numbers of meetings out of school time – and this will not be reflected in salaries! No wonder there is universal opposition to these proposals in the teaching profession. This Bill, rushed through Parliament before the gaping holes in the fabric became apparent, is likely to do more harm to education in this country than any measure since the Revised Code of 1862. Teachers will again be completely in the power of headteachers with no right of appeal. Unfortunately, not all headteachers are above being corrupted by such absolute power. This is a Bill to encourage tyranny and a return to Victorian conditions as well as values.

I think many teachers would welcome an agreed statement of the range and limits of their contractual duties, worked out through consultation. But this can only be done successfully if all parties to the negotiations are genuinely committed to improving education (rather than making a virtue out of a cost-cutting exercise), understand what is involved in the process of education and respect the work which teachers do. Then teachers' duties would be accompanied by the right to protection from exploitation of their goodwill, so that they would be entitled to support in the classroom and guaranteed time for preparation and marking during the school day, as well as having reasonable limits on class size and the amount of their own time which they are expected to give up to school matters.

The Secretary of State has also indicated that he favours a structure which would divide teachers into more grades and give extra payments to 'good' teachers. Now this may sound reasonable – surely virtue should be rewarded – but how can this work in practice? Who will decide who are the 'good' teachers in any school? Will it be the headteacher? Or will this be another task for the Inspectorate, who are, like the teachers, themselves overworked and underpaid, considering the responsibilities which they are called upon to shoulder and the extended hours which they work. This is another of those proposals which seems admirable, but appears more half-baked (or should one say half-Bakered?) as one examines it.

There has also been an announcement of the intention to impose a national core curriculum. Such a notion is not, on the surface, unattractive. Surely all our children should have equal opportunities, wherever they go to school. But primary schools already have a basic core: according to HMI this is not the weakness. The weakness is in the lack of those very investigative approaches applauded by industrialists (see page 142). And when this is put forward by a minister in a government which has applauded the lowest spending by local authorities, and has advocated the exclusion of 'fringe' subjects like music and the arts from the curriculum, advising that these should be provided by parents privately, it begins to have a more sinister aspect.

The Revised Code of 1862 was designed to ensure that children achieved a recommended minimum standard and, as outlined earlier, it had a devastating effect on education throughout England and Wales. The way to achieve a national curriculum that represents a real educational advance would be to draw on the experience and understanding of properly-paid teachers throughout the country; to consult with parents and other interested parties, and work towards the promotion of agreed educational aims by the use of those methods and strategies that were found to be most successful in the development of children's learning. Above all there would need to be the honest intention to provide adequate finance. Yet this is precisely what government has opposed. Can such a radical improvement be achieved on the cheap? Obviously it cannot; nor can it be enforced by *diktat* from above.

What can be done, however, is to reduce the maintained system of education to such a pitiable level that all those parents who can possibly afford it will be forced to send their children into private education while the government creams off an elite which will be sent to the 20 City Technical Colleges which they are planning to set up. The rest of the nation will be in a complete no-hope situation with only the dole queues to come! What a wicked and frustrating waste of human talent in the years ahead. What a formula for social disaster!

What kind of future?

If a minority of pupils are creamed off and given access to scientific and technological education which will fit them for the higher reaches of employment, while the majority are to be allowed to participate only in a minimal national curriculum in schools operating at the lowest possible cost, the aim of which is to ensure they can read, write and reckon, what kind of future can they anticipate? Are they to be the servicers of a fast-food Britain which is a vast tourist centre, an off-shore island, with our youth cooking the pizzas and hamburgers and washing up the glasses? Or will we ensure that all our children are educated to be citizens of an advanced technological state which offers them a civilised standard of living and equal oportunities for fulfilment?

The utmost pressure needs to be exerted to end the shift towards the privatisation of education and the down-grading of the maintained system. Greater participation in education by parents is being encouraged at all levels; this is the time for them to act. The expression of concern by parents and teachers in London when the ILEA was threatened with abolition in 1985 certainly had a positive effect. What is needed now is public pressure to bring about a transfer of resources from areas which do not improve the lives of the mass of people, like the growing expenditure on arms and military equipment, into areas like education which are vital for the future of the nation. It is our children and grandchildren who will have to pay for Baker's Bill. It is their futures which are being mortgaged.

Postscript: Learning to enjoy school

The choice of a school for your children is of great importance. The majority of parents choose the primary school which is closest to home. Some parents even choose homes which are near to particular schools. Of course, if you have a particular requirement, such as wanting your child to have denominational religious instruction, then you would want to find a particular kind of school. If your child has special needs then this should have been discussed with your health visitor and doctor, and advice given on the kind of treatment and schooling that he or she would find most beneficial.

In most cases the school closest to home is the best choice. There are many advantages, not the least of which is that your child grows up within a group of school friends, many of whom are likely to live in walking distance. It is better for a small child to be able to walk to school rather than have to be transported, and for the distance not to be too great, especially in bad weather. It makes it easier too, for children and parents to be involved in after-school activities of various kinds, which encourages their participation in the full life of the school. Schools can also help young parents to get to know other families in the neighbourhood, which can be useful for baby-sitting arrangements, and so on.

But what if there is no school very close to home or you have the choice of several? Or what if the closest school has a bad reputation – you may have heard from other parents that they have chosen not to send their children there? First, do not be influenced by local tales: visit the school yourself. Prejudice against it might be based on something which happened a long time ago, and the school could be quite different now. Or the tales might have no foundation in fact. Or your expectations of a school might even be different from those of your neighbours, so do make an appointment and have a look.

If after taking a look, you are still unsure, then the place to contact is the local education office, for they will be able to give you a list of schools within a certain radius of your home. Each school now has to publish a booklet giving its aims, objectives and policies, and these will give you some insight into the differences between schools. The next step will be to visit the schools, preferably taking your child with you, because the attitude of staff and pupils to you and your child will also give you an idea of the ethos of the school.

How does one judge a school? One can tell a great deal by first impressions: not of the exterior of the building, for many good schools exist in old and forbidding buildings, but by the way you are greeted as you enter. Is it bleak, or is there a lively array of children's work and interesting notices? Is it colourful and friendly? How are you and your child treated: as welcome guests, or as a nuisance to be suffered? How are the other pupils treated? Would you be happy for your own child to be talked to and dealt with as they are? Are the classrooms busy, with children doing things and talking to each other, or are they sitting silently working from textbooks? As you go around classrooms, can you see a progression of work between that of the five-year-olds and that of the oldest classes? Are there plenty of books and equipment *being used*? It is not a good sign when equipment is all in perfect condition and kept out of reach in cupboards. It does keep it in tip-top condition, but the children don't learn anything from its use!

How do the children in the school treat one another? How do they treat you and your child? Are they friendly and informative? Can they explain what they are doing? Is the children's work on display varied, showing a broad curriculum? And is the display well done, showing that children's work is valued in the school? Is there evidence of practical work in all areas of the curriculum? Are children getting opportunities for investigation or are they all the time being told what is right? All these are questions for you to find answers to, and to check against the school's published policy. Here is where you can check that the hidden curriculum does match the stated one. The kind of playgrounds provided for the children are another indication of the school: have they been made brighter and more interesting, or are they as bleak as they were in Queen Victoria's day?

Having found the school you would like to send your child to, you may have to fill in an application form, because with numbers of applicants rising now in many areas, schools cannot automatically take all of them. If applicable, do give any special reasons for wanting that particular school. Once you hear that your child will have a place in the school, you could then try to arrange for him or her to spend one or two morning or afternoon sessions there, perhaps with you at first, so that the child becomes familiar with the school before starting. Some schools do, in any case, organise such sessions, perhaps combined with a chat to parents about school policy, and you should try to attend this, because all sorts of questions can be cleared up immediately.

Preparations for school

During this time you will have been preparing your child for school. This is less a question of formal preparations, of teaching your child to read or write, than of preparing him or her to start school with confidence. The best way to help a child to learn to read is to read to him or her, in circumstances pleasurable to both of you.

The most important preparation for school is to help your child to be as independent as possible. Before starting school the child should be able to dress and undress. One cause of great distress in children starting school is that when they have to undress for physical activities, if they have never had to dress themselves, they cannot conceive of ever getting back into their clothes. If they are not dressed, they can see no way of ever going home again and they are overtaken by hysteria. I have known children who have refused to take part in any PE, and usually found this to be the reason. They will also feel more comfortable if they are used to being seen in their underwear by other people and don't experience this for the first time on starting school. Life is easier for them (and their teachers!) if they have clothes with front fastenings, jumpers with enough headroom for putting off and on, and shoes which they can fasten themselves. As mentioned earlier, they will be happier for having their clothes marked so that they do not get mislaid. They need to be able to manage their own lavatory visits and handwashing, so these too should be practised at home first.

Another area of strain for small children is the dinner hall, which is inevitably much noisier than anything they have experienced. The food may be strange, and the children will probably be given some choice because this is now the policy of many schools. Try to encourage your child to eat a range of foods and offer some choices so that he or she will be able to take such decisions in his or her stride as well. Make sure he or she has experience of eating with a knife and fork too, because this will be expected in school.

Of course, if children have attended a nursery class or playgroup, some of these hurdles will already have been surmounted. They will be used to being left with other adults and lots of children. But if your child has not had this experience, then you should arrange to leave him or her with another mother and child, or with a group of children, to become more confident about being left, and to develop a sense of security in knowing that you will come back.

Many schools now encourage mothers or fathers to stay with their children for a while when they begin school. Sneaking off while the child's attention is distracted is *not* encouraged because your unexpected absence would then be a shock to the child. If your child cries and clings to you, be patient. If this continues for more than one or two days, look critically at your early morning routine: is there something you are doing which is causing concern to the child? Are you rushing preparations for school, chivvying him or her at breakfast? If so, get up half an hour earlier, and make things more relaxed: it could make all the difference. Or could it be that it is you who are fearful of leaving the child, and communicating this anxiety? Another cause for distress is if there is a younger child at home who is going to be alone with you, and careful attention to the older child can overcome this jealousy. If there has been any family tension, any death or sudden illness, or disappearance of a familiar figure, then the child is going to feel worried in case this should happen to you too. Reassure your child about this and, if you can, let the teacher know so that he or she can be reassuring and treat the problem with understanding. Be guided by the staff; if they suggest that you should say goodbye and go, then do this even if the child cries. There are some children who never seem able to settle in the classroom until their mothers or fathers have left. Some children come in more easily with their fathers. But usually a secure child, when feeling ready to be left, will say something like 'You can go now, mummy'!

Some schools also introduce children to full-time schooling gently, beginning with the mornings only. Or it may be possible for you to take your child home for lunches in the early days of schooling. You may well find that you will very soon be told by the child, quite definitely, that he or she no longer welcomes the interruption to the school day!

One most important thing is always to be punctual at going-home time – even a few minutes lateness can result in an over-wrought, tearful, and sometimes hostile child. This leads to you making guilty reparations of an over-indulgent nature, and can encourage your child into those paths of manipulation that are better avoided. As well as the effect on your child, lateness is very inconsiderate. Teachers might well have children of their own to collect, and your lateness could be a cause of great inconvenience for them and distress for their children as well.

If there should be a day when you realise that, through some misadventure, you are not going to be at the school at the proper time, then do telephone and leave a message for the teacher to that effect. Then the child can be prepared and the whole situation is calmer.

When you talk to a young child about school, a positive attitude on your part will be all-important. If school has been held up before the child as a kind of bogey – 'You won't be able to do that when you go to school', or 'Your teacher will soon put an end to that!' – you have made a rod for your own back by inducing anxiety about school in the child. But if you have been pointing out the new activities in which the child will be sharing, and how enjoyable these will be, then the child will begin school with eagerness and enthusiasm. The kind of behaviour suitable to members of large groups in school will be learned easily by most children who come to school with the right kind of preparation and without anxiety.

Children often find it difficult to put into words their experiences at school, especially when they are asked questions. The usual answer to 'What did you do at school today?' is 'I played'. Because small children get very tired when they first begin school, it is best not to press for explicit answers at this point. Very often it will be in the bath, at a meal, or at bed-time, when the child is feeling more relaxed, that it will all come pouring out – 'Do you know what David did, Mummy?' or 'Jane isn't my friend any more' – and soon, so often that you may get rather tired of hearing it, 'Miss says . . .'!

People make schools what they are

When a child begins school, he or she will meet a large number of new adults. As well as the teachers, there will also be the schoolkeeper, the school secretary and the support staff, also known as 'helpers'. They all make very important contributions to the friendliness and atmosphere of the school.

The schoolkeeper, who most small pupils believe owns the school, is responsible for its physical condition – no small responsibility when one thinks of the number of people using the building daily – and for the cleaners who work both before and after school.

The school secretary is involved in every facet of school life, collects dinner money, arranges medical lists, and is in and out of classrooms all day. She (for it usually is a woman, except in secondary schools) is a very important samaritan for a small child in difficulties – as indeed is the schoolkeeper.

The support staff, or women helpers, work in classrooms, especially with the youngest children. They put out equipment, keep it clean and in working order, and take care of the pencils, paper and paints. They help children to dress and undress, help with the school milk, clear up messes of all kinds and do 101 jobs which are of help to teachers. They also help to look after children in the playground during break times, and take care of the sick and wounded. I have seen a school helper organise a playground with perhaps 200 children into organised games, without shouting at the children, without the use of a whistle or a bell, and ensure that they all enjoyed their games with a minimum of hassle of any kind, something not every teacher could do as well. Of course, she was able to do this because of her good relationship with the children and their respect for her.

As well as all this, helpers are increasingly being asked to participate in the learning process, sitting with children doing puzzles and talking with them, listening to them read, playing games, intervening in disputes and working very much in partnership with the teachers. In the nursery class the nursery assistant will have similar responsibilities.

Also soon familiar to the children will be the kitchen staff, supervised by the cook, who have to be at the school very early in the morning to prepare the food for the day. They serve the children their meals and have to remember which child is not allowed which foods.

Some schools also have play centres or after-school clubs, which extend the school day, and these also employ separate staffs (sometimes these include one or more of the school's teachers or helpers), under the leadership of a supervisor. They provide a variety of activities for children, including visits, and maintain very informal and friendly relations with them. Once again, these staffs have to be very skilled at organising large numbers of children into positive play activities.

The doctor, the dentist, the photographer and the school nurse

A lot of small children become nervous when any one of these four appears. Strangely, there are some children who make more fuss about having their picture taken than they do about seeing the doctor or dentist. But a lot of tears can be avoided if parents, when they know the school is to be visited by one or other of these, talk to their children and reassure them that nothing untoward is likely to happen. It is a good idea to accompany your child when he or she is to be seen by the school doctor. The school doctor specialises in children, and, since GPs are usually very busy, they are good people with whom to raise any health problems. Often the school doctor will already know you and your child from clinic or nursery, and the relationship can be extended through the school.

When the dentist visits the school, it is normally just to look at the children's teeth. It is important for children to know that no treatment will be carried out at the school. And it is a good idea for them to get used to the dentist looking at their teeth.

School photographs are nearly always well taken and treasured by parents, grandparents and other relatives. But if your child doesn't want a picture taken one year, the best thing is to forget it – there will be another chance next year!

Of all four, the school nurse is the person who your child will see most often. She will carry out tests for sight and hearing, do hygiene checks from time to time, and she will probably be the person to deliver the shampoo, if and when your child picks up the dreaded head lice. Do remember that lice seem to prefer clean heads – infestation is not a sign of careless or dirty parents and no one will condemn you if it should happen. It is all much less hush-hush than it was when you went to school.

Your child's work

At any school gate at home-time, young children can be seen proudly displaying pieces of their own work, paintings, models and special occasion cards which they have made. These represent hard work and real achievement, but sometimes they are not valued as such by parents who judge them as finished products. They are not that; they are symptoms of a process: they have been thrown up in the course of the child's learning activities, and the greatest encouragement for children to go on learning is their parents' pleasure, appreciation, interest and encouragement. In any case, your child's work is unique and can tell you a great deal about the way his or her mind works, if you take the trouble to look at it with care. A lot of children's art is fascinating. A piece of work which has been thought about and crafted with care has its own beauty, whether the artist is five or 45. There is nothing sadder for a teacher who asks a little child 'Did Mummy like your picture?' than to be told by a small voice, 'She didn't like it. She threw it away'. My response when this happened, as would probably be that of most teachers, was a matter-of-fact 'Oh well, never mind. This one is lovely and I am going to put it on our classroom wall for everyone to see', but both of us knew that this was a poor consolation.

At some point, your child will come home with a reading book. Please remember that learning to read is not a race, it doesn't really matter whether the child down the road brought a book home earlier or later than your child. Of course you want to be reassured that your son or daughter is as bright and capable of learning as the next child, but the kind of pressure you put on your child by communicating disappointment that he or she is not always *the first* in every field is likely to be very counter-productive. Anxiety can cause a kind of mental paralysis which prevents learning, and it really is of no great significance whether someone is reading at four-and-a-half, five, or six, so long as he or she does learn to enjoy reading. Try to avoid worrying about climbing the book ladder from Book One onwards. Instead ensure that your child gets a variety of simple books to read. Read the books together – and don't be concerned if he or she appears to be memorising the book: very many children use this technique early in the process of learning to read. It is quite legitimate and exemplifies the phenomenal memory found in children. Don't worry about correcting mistakes, most learners will correct their own mistakes quite quickly, especially if you in your turn read the book correctly to the child.

If by the time your child is coming up to seven years, you do feel that there are reading problems or other learning difficulties which do not seem to be clearing up, then go and speak to the teacher or the headteacher.

At parents' evenings you will have an opportunity to see your child's work, the work of other children in the class, and probably the work of other classes as well. When you look at a child's books, files, folders, or whatever their work is collected in, remember that not all the work you see will be finished work. Most of it will be produced in the process of learning, and often be first drafts. There will be some beautifully finished work on display, but not every piece is going to be finished to that level, otherwise the children would be spending most of their time copying and re-copying two or three pieces of work. This would not be a very profitable way of using their time, unless we were training them to become clerks in some Victorian-style office. If you think of producing a piece of writing, a letter or an article, yourself, then you know that you might do several drafts before achieving the final product. Mistakes can provide a lot of learning, so do not expect to see everything done perfectly. It is the continuing process of education which is important, although I think every child also needs some finished products to show with pride.

School reports are sent home at intervals which will depend upon the custom of the school and the LEA. These vary considerably, and many primary schools no longer set annual examinations or give percentage marks for each child. Some might give grades for different curriculum areas, but the best will give you a more detailed description of the child's strengths and weaknesses, and the progress being made. Details of attendance and punctuality are usually included. If children are frequently late, or have a large number of avoidable absences, then they are losing a lot of time at school. This is bound to affect academic progress adversely and it is then up to parents to review the situation self-critically and see how it can best be remedied. If the report indicates less progress than one might have hoped, there is nothing to be gained by conveying disappointment to the child when there has been unjustified loss of time.

The present and the future

The time a child spends at school is important in itself, in the here and now, and it should be enjoyed to the fullest, for its own sake. Childhood is not just a training period for adulthood. All phases of life should be lived fully, each in its own time. But what happens to us in childhood does affect our adult lives in many ways. There is a great deal of information now about the importance of feeding our children correctly so that they should not suffer diseases of malnutrition. We would not put them into too small shoes and deform their feet. It has even been suggested that smoking and alcohol intake during pregnancy may result in hyperactive infants who might themselves, later in their lives, have a greater tendency to form addictive habits. But there is less advice on how to avoid imposing psychological problems on our offspring. How can we avoid patterns of behaviour that might inhibit their development both in childhood and maturity?

While it is no part of this book to discuss family relationships and their psychological consequences, the bonds between children and their parents are very deep and can be unwittingly twisted by a failure on the part of parents to give the support, encouragement and approval, when due, to the future man or woman emerging from the chrysalis of the child. Children's efforts should not be ignored, derided, patronised, shown to be a nuisance or an unwelcome distraction, but welcomed and discussed. Nor should our response ever be an uncritical 'Oh, lovely, darling' because that is the most patronising response of all. It is necessary to give real consideration, and make an assessment of the evidence of effort in the process, and constructively criticise the product. There are times when it might be difficult to understand what was in the mind of children, and perhaps they have forgotten, or can't express in words what they had intended. But one always find something interesting in any piece of work.

Very many adults, reflecting upon their childhood and their relations with their parents, will recall the frustration they experienced because of their inability to meet their parents' expectations, however hard they tried. 'I never seemed able to please my father', or 'My mother was always disappointed because' – and there follows any one of a variety of causes. In my own childhood I remember being always aware of my mother's disappointment that I lacked the physical grace of a cousin, slightly older than myself, who was one of those little girls who always stayed neat and tidy, seemed never to tear her clothes (which was fortunate for me because they were usually passed on to me!), and always looked presentable, while I never managed to stay clean and tidy for long. Luckily it did not stop my cousin and me from being good friends, but it certainly gave me a considerable sense of physical inferiority and a yearning for an elegance which is beyond my achievement!

Whose schools are they?

In law, the school belongs to the local education authority which, together with the government, is responsible for the provision of education for all children between five and 16 years. While the head and teaching staff are employed at a particular school, it is their school. The school will be their school for the non-teaching staff – helpers, kitchen staff, cleaners, school-keeper and school secretary. For all the children attending, it will also be their school. While your children attend the school, it is also your school. In and around each school, there is a school community. Just as it is important for children that their parents support them in their learning, so it is important for them to feel united with their parents in an interest in, and support for, the activities of the school.

During the time your child attends a primary school you are eligible to be a parent governor (unless you are an employee of the education authority), a member of the parent-teacher association (PTA), if one exists in the school, or, if you have the time, and if the school requests it, a voluntary helper in the school. The school governors are appointed in various ways. As well as those elected by the parents, some are appointed by the local education authority, some by the local council, and others can be nominated by a university. Teachers elect teacher governors, and in some areas there is also a representative elected by the non-teaching staff. In the Inner London Education Authority governing bodies are also required to have representatives from minority ethnic groups. Of course the job of the governors is to take care of the whole school and all its staff and pupils. They have a responsibility for appointing staff and in some areas even share the task of appointing the headteacher with the members of the local education authority.

One often hears parents spoken of as if there were a unanimity of outlook among them, but this is far from true. There is a wide range of opinions and completely different expectations to be found among any group of parents. The governors and staff can only satisfy some of those expectations, but it is through the parent governors that other parents' opinions can be brought into the light of a governors' meeting and receive consideration. If a parent has a problem and doesn't know who to raise it with, then the parent governor is probably the best person to consult. Many governors' meetings are open to observers, providing a good opportunity to find out how they work.

School associations and PTAs are other channels through which parents can express their opinions to the school, and their meetings can often be used as a sounding board on numerous questions. But if they are to be representative, then as many parents as possible need to attend. There are often complaints that such organisations are unrepresentative, because one group of parents is on the committee which decides everything. The only way to overcome this situation is for lots of people to be ready to help with the work and see that decisions are democratically arrived at. And there is a lot of work; nowadays schools rely increasingly on their voluntary funds for buying necessities which can no longer be purchased out of their allowances because of the effects of government education cuts. The voluntary fund, or school fund, is made up of all the money raised by parents, staff and children, and is not part of the school's official financing. All kinds of activities are arranged by parents and teachers, and their success depends upon the support of the main body of parents.

A school is one of the places where people of all kinds from different backgrounds are drawn together and can mix in an enterprise in which they all have a tremendous investment – their children. Children get very involved in preparations for sales, dances and performances, and the participation of their own parents in these school activities is a source of great satisfaction to them. It forges important links between home and school. They can proudly show the school to their parents, and are proud to show their parents to their friends and teachers.

Just as there is now much more realisation in schools of the valuable things all children bring into the school from their own experience and cultural background, so there is also greater appreciation of what parents can offer the schools. A growing number of schools make their own books, and the concept of children as authors has become widespread. Parents as authors is another valuable idea, because parents, who have a wide range of experience, and who may have been brought up in other countries, can produce stories and factual accounts of their own early lives which the children love to read. I know of several small children whose enthusiasm for reading and writing grew from a book made at home – sometimes involving other members of the family as well, for grandparents very often have the most interesting tales to tell.

Schools have changed a great deal in the last 20 to 30 years, and there is a much greater understanding that education is a co-operative effort involving the child, the child's parents and family, and the school. Most schools are much less formal in their relations with parents than they used to be, because it has become clearer that children learn better when there is positive family involvement. It is also more satisfying for parents and teachers when there are closer and more friendly relations between them; they have a bond, a common interest in the progress of the children. So parents too can learn to enjoy school, if they enter with confidence and enthusiasm!

Mrs Pinder is getting dressed

Select Bibliography

Almay,M., with Chittenden and Miller. *Young Children's Thinking* (1961), Teachers' College Press, Columbia University, New York.

Ashton-Warner, Sylvia. *Spinster* (1958), Secker and Warburg, London.

Assessment of Performance Unit. *Language Performance in Schools, 1986,* HMSO, London.

Assessment of Performance Unit. *Language Testing 1979 – 83,* HMSO, London.

Auld, Robin, Q.C., *Report of the Public Inquiry into the William Tyndale Junior and Infants Schools* (1976), ILEA, London.

Axtell,J.L. *Educational Writings of John Locke* (1968), Cambridge University Press.

Badley,J.H. *Bedales* (1923), Methuen, London

Blackie, John. *Changing the Primary School* (1974), Macmillan, London.

Bruner, Jerome. *Towards a Theory of Instruction* (1966), Harvard University Press, Cambridge, Mass.

Burt, Cyril. *The Education of Illiterate Adults* (1945), British Journal of Educational Psychology, February.

Buxton, Laurie. *Do You Panic About Maths?* (1981), Heinemann Educational, London.

Clay, Marie. *Reading – The Patterning of Complex Behaviour* (1979), Heinemann Educational, London.

Clegg, Arthur. *About our Schools* (1980), Basil Blackwell, Oxford.

Cockcroft Committee. *Mathematics Counts,* Report of the Committee of Inquiry into the Teaching of Mathematics in Schools, under the Chairmanship of Dr W.H.Cockcroft (1982), HMSO, London.

Cox,C.B. and Dyson,A.E. *Black Paper Two: The Crisis in Education* (1969), Critical Quarterly Society.

Crump,G. *Bedales Since the War* (1936), Chapman and Hall, London.

Curry,W.B. *Dartington Hall* (1958), Phoenix House, London.

Davies, Y. *Picture Stories,* edited by Cary Bazalgette (1986), British Film Institute, London.

Department of Education and Science. *Education in Schools - a consultative document* (1977), HMSO, London.

217

Department of Education and Science. *Primary Education in England* (1981), HMSO, London.

Department of Education and Science. *The School Curriculum* (1981), HMSO, London.

Dewey, John. *Experience and Education* (1938) Macmillan, New York.

Dewey, John. *The School and Society* (1910), University of Chicago Press.

Dewey, John. *The Child and the Curriculum*, (1956), University of Chicago Press.

Dunkel,H.B. *Herbart and Herbartianism: An Educational Ghost Story* (1970), University of Chicago Press.

Edmunds,L.F. *Rudolf Steiner Education* (1962), Rudolf Steiner Press, London.

Ellis,T. et al. *William Tyndale, The Teachers' Story* (1976), Writers and Readers, London.

Ensor,B. *Education for the New Era* (1920), vol 1, No 1 January.

Fowler,T. *Locke's Conduct of the Understanding* (1901), Clarendon Press, Oxford.

Froebel,F. *Pedagogics of the Kindergarten*, translated by Josephine Jarvis (1899), E.Arnold, London.

Froebel,F. *The Education of Man*, translated by W.N.Hailmann (1902), D.Appleton-Century, New York and London.

Froebel,F. *Autobiography*, translated by Emilie Michaelis and H.Keatle Morre (1903), Sonnenschein and Co, London.

Galton,M., Simon,B., Croll,P. *Inside the Primary Classroom* (1980), Routledge and Kegan Paul, London.

Galton,M. and Simon,B. (eds) *Progress and Performance in the Primary Classroom* (1980), Routledge and Kegan Paul, London.

Gerhardt, Lydia. *Moving and Knowing* (1973), Prentice Hall, New Jersey.

Gordon,P. and Lawton,D. *Curriculum Change in the Nineteenth and Twentieth Centuries* (1978), Hodder and Stoughton, London.

Gretton,J. and Jackson,M. *William Tyndale: Collapse of a School or a System?* (1976), George Allen and Unwin, London.

Gribble, David. *Considering Children* (1985), Dorling Kindersley, London.

Gulbenkian Report. *The Arts in Schools* (1982), Calouste Gulbenkian Foundation.

Harlen, Wynn. *New Trends in Primary School Science Education* (1983), UNESCO.

Harlen, Wynn. *Does Content Matter in Primary Science?* (1978), School Science Review, Vol 59, June.

Hayward,F.H. *The Secret of Herbart: An Essay on the Science of Education* (1907), Watts and Co., London.

Herbart,J.F. *The Science of Education* (1892), George Routledge, London, 1924.

Herbart,J.F. *The Application of Psychology to the Science of Education* (1898), Swann Sonnenschein and Co., London.

Hilsum,S. and Cane,B.S. *The Teacher's Day* (1981), National Foundation for Educational Research, London.

HM Inspectorate. *Primary Education in England* (1978), HMSO, London.

HM Inspectorate. *Report on the Effects of Local Authority Expenditure Policies on Education* (1985), HMSO, London.

Holmes,G. *The Idiot Teacher* (1977), Faber and Faber, London.

Holt, John. *How Children Learn* (1968), Pitman, London.

Jameson, Kenneth. *Pre-School and Infant Art* (1968), Studio Vista, Eastbourne.

Kamin, Leon J. *The Science and Politics of I.Q.* (1974), Penguin, London.

Krutetskii,V.A. *The Psychology of Mathematical Abilities in School-children.* Translated from Russian by Joan Teller, edited by Jeremy Kilpatrick and Izaak Wirszup (1976), University of Chicago Press.

Kuhn, Thomas. *Structure of Scientific Revolutions* (1962), University of Chicago Press.

Lawrence, Elizabeth. *The Origins and Growth of Modern Education* (1970), Penguin, London.

Lilley,I.M. *Friedrich Froebel – a Selection from his Writings* (1967), Chicago University Press.

McCabe, J. *Robert Owen* (1920), Watts and Co., London.

Maclure,J.S. *Educational Documents, England and Wales, 1816–1967,* (1968) Methuen, London.

Masterman, Len. *Teaching the Media* (1985), Comedia, London.

Ministry of Education. *The Story of Post-War School Building* (1957), Pamphlet No 33, HMSO, London.

Montessori, Maria. *The Montessori Method* (1937), Heinemann, London.

National Union of Teachers. *The Struggle for Education 1870–1970,* (1970), N.U.T., London.

Neill,A.S. *That Dreadful School,* (1937), Herbert Jenkins, London.

Neill,A.S. *The Free Child* (1953), Herbert Jenkins, London.

Newland, Mary and Rubens, Maurice. *Some Functions of Art in the Primary School* (1983), ILEA, London.

Newsom Committee. *Half Our Future:* Report on Secondary Education, chaired by Mr. John Newsom (1963), Central Advisory Council for Education, London.

Owen, Robert. *A New View of Society, and Report to the County of Lanark.* Ed. V.A.C. Gatrell (1970), Penguin, London.

Pearson,E. *Trends In School Design* (1972), Macmillan, London.

Pestalozzi,J.H. *Leonard and Gertrude,* translated by Eva Channing (1895), D.C.Heath and Co, Boston.

Pestalozzi,J.H. *Letters on Early Education: addressed to J.P. Greaves* (1827), Sherwood, Gilbert and Piper, London.

Piaget, Jean. *The Growth of Logical Thinking* (1966), Routledge and Kegan Paul, London.

Pilkington Report. *The Primary School, An Environment for Education* (1967), Pilkington Research Unit, University of Liverpool.

Pinder,R. *Pupil Observers in one London Primary School* (1984), Forum, Vol 27, Number 1, Autumn.

Plowden Report. *Children and their Primary Schools:* A Report by the Central Advisory Council for Education (England), chaired by Lady Plowden, (1967), HMSO, London.

Pollard,H.M. *Pioneers of Popular Education, 1760–1850* (1956), Murray, London.

Quick,R.H. *Essays on Educational Reformers* (1890), Longman, London.

Rousseau,J.J. *Emile, or Education,* translated by Barbara Foxley (1933), J.M.Dent, London.

Rousseau,J.J. *The Minor Educational Writings of Jean Jacques Rousseau,* selected and translated by William Boyd (1911), Blackie, Glasgow.

Rubinstein,D. (Ed). *Education and Equality* (1979), Penguin, London.

Russell, Bertrand. *On Education* (1926), George Allen and Unwin, London.

Scher, Anna and Verrall, Charles. *100+ Ideas for Drama* (1977), Heinemann Educational, London.

Schools Council. *The Practical Curriculum* (1981), Schools Council Working Paper 70, Methuen Educational, London.

Seaborne,M. *Primary School Design* (1971), Routledge and Kegan Paul, London.

Seaborne,M. and Lowe,R. *The English School: Its Architecture and Organization. Vol II, 1870–1970* (1977), Routledge and Kegan Paul, London.

Selleck,R.J.W. *The New Education: The English Background, 1870–1914* (1968), Pitman, London.

Selleck,R.J.W. *English Primary Education and the Progressives, 1914–39* (1972), Routledge and Kegan Paul, London.

Sharp,R. and Green,H. *Education and Social Control* (1975), Routledge and Kegan Paul, London.

Silber,K. *Pestalozzi* (1960), Routledge and Kegan Paul, London.

Simon,B. *Intelligence, Psychology and Education* (1971), Lawrence and Wishart, London.

Simon,B. *The Radical Tradition in Education in Britain* (1972), Lawrence and Wishart, London.

Simon,B. and Willcocks,J. (eds) *Research and Practice in the Primary Classroom* (1981), Routledge and Kegan Paul, London.

Simon, Joan. *Education and Society in Tudor England* (1960), Cambridge University Press.

Skemp, Richard. *Mathematics Teaching* (1976), December.

Smail,W.M. *Quintilian on Education* (1938), Oxford University Press.

Smith, Frank. *Understanding Reading* (1971), Holt, Rinehart and Winston, Eastbourne.

Smith, Frank. *Reading* (1978), Cambridge University Press.

Steiner, Rudolf. *The Story of My Life* (1928), Anthroposophical Publishing Co, London.

Stewart, Jan. *The Making of the Primary School* (1986), Open University Press.

Stewart,W.A.C. *The Educational Innovators* (1968), Macmillan, London.

Stewart,W.A.C. *Quakers and Education* (1953), Epworth Press, London.

UNESCO. *John Amos Comenius on Education* (1967), with introduction by Jean Piaget, Teachers' College Press, Columbia University, New York.

Van der Eyken,W. and Turner, B. *Adventures in Education* (1969), Penguin, London.

Watson, Foster. *English Grammar Schools to 1660* (1968), Frank Cass, London.

Whitbread, Nanette. *The Evolution of the Nursery-Infant School* (1972), Routledge and Kegan Paul, London.

Williams,A.M. *Johann Friedrich Herbart* (1911), Blackie, Glasgow.

Wright, Nigel. *Progress in Education* (1977), Croom Helm, London.

Index

For types of education, e.g. elementary, child-centred, *see* education.